CULTURE SHOCK

A SURVIVAL GUIDE FOR TEENS

IGNITING AN INTEGRITY AND PURITY REVOLUTION

BY JULIE HIRAMINE
WITH THE GENERATIONS OF VIRTUE TEAM

Standard PUBLISHING
Bringing The Word to Life

Cincinnati, Ohio

Published by Standard Publishing, Cincinnati, Ohio
www.standardpub.com

Copyright © 2011 Generations of Virtue

Printed in: United States of America
Acquisitions editor: Robert Irvin
Cover design: Scott Ryan
Interior design: Thinkpen Design, Inc., www.thinkpendesign.com

All Scripture quotations, unless otherwise indicated, are taken from the *HOLY BIBLE, NEW INTERNATIONAL VERSION*®. *NIV*®. Copyright © 1973, 1978, 1984, 2011 by Biblica, Inc.™ Used by permission. All rights reserved worldwide. Scripture quotations marked (*AMP*) are taken from the *Amplified*® *Bible*. Copyright © 1954, 1958, 1962, 1965, 1987 by The Lockman Foundation. Used by permission. (www.Lockman.org) All rights reserved. Scripture quotations marked (*The Message*) are taken from *The Message*. Copyright © by Eugene H. Peterson 1993, 1994, 1995, 1996, 2000, 2001, 2002. Used by permission of NavPress Publishing Group. Scripture quotations marked (*NLT*) are taken from the Holy Bible, *New Living Translation*. Copyright © 1996, 2004. Used by permission of Tyndale House Publishers, Inc., Wheaton, Illinois 60189. All rights reserved.

ISBN 978-0-7847-3305-9

16 15 14 13 12 11   1 2 3 4 5 6 7 8 9

CONTENTS

★ **START** HERE ★

Skim the magazine racks, flip on the TV, or make a few clicks on the Internet and you get smacked in the face with it. Hypersexuality, obscenity, perversion. All aggressively marketed directly at you. Add in the world's definitions of tolerance, acceptance, spirituality, and truth and the lines between right and wrong start getting pretty fuzzy.

Riding the waves of life as a teen is tricky enough if you only have to keep up with school and your relationships. Dealing with peer pressure, gossip, technology, and media's constant flow makes those waves a whole lot stormier. And somehow in the middle of this you are supposed to discover who you are and what you've been created to do. How in the world can you do all that and keep your head above water?

Culture Shock is a five-session interactive teen event designed to empower you to take a stand against the toxic tide we all find ourselves immersed in. This survival guide was put together by people traveling the same roads of life you are now on. We've been there; we know what it is to struggle. Some of us are just out of our teens, some have been on the road a bit longer; some are married now and some are single. But we're all dedicated to honoring God with lives built on integrity and purity. And we're convinced there is only one Way and one Truth, no matter what lies Satan tries to feed us.

The God who made the world and came down to save it is the same God who wants to use you as part of his perfect plan. He has an amazing design for romance, relationships, and every aspect of your life. As you learn to stand firm on his Word, you'll find yourself strengthened by the unstoppable power of the cross and see your world changed by the power of Jesus' name.

We hope the devotional thoughts, questions, and Bible studies in these pages encourage you to be intentional about your pursuit of purity and help you develop strategies for keeping your integrity intact. Whether you use this book on your own or with a Culture Shock small group, be committed to being honest about where you are and what needs to happen next in your life for you to take hold of God's plan for you.

It's time. It's time for you to step up. **It's time for us all to shock the culture** with our devotion to the one true God. Let's go!

THE GENERATIONS OF VIRTUE TEAM

Have questions or want to keep in touch with our team? Head over to www.generationsof virtue.org for more. And, to stay in touch with other world changers, visit our blog at www.apuregeneration.com. We want to hear from you! ☆

PART ONE

CINDERELLA LIED, SUPERMAN DIED

Songs, television, movies, online content. They have a massive impact on how we see ourselves and others, how we make decisions, and how we spend our time. We have allowed media to speak into our lives so loudly, it has actually begun to shape who we are, the decisions we make, and how we live.

Now, this wouldn't be an issue if all media taught us about was Christianity or how to become more like Jesus. But we all know that its messages go far from that. We have to realize that our generation will continue to be influenced by the media machine until we understand, deep in our hearts, that our character is shaped by whomever or whatever we allow to enter into our minds.

How much time do you spend every day watching TV or a movie or on social networking or chatting with friends? Now compare that amount with how much time you spend with God every day. Who do you think has the greater influence on your life?

If we had any idea how much we were being impacted by media, would we still consume it so easily? Although it might be a little challenging, we want you to dive into this study and see, maybe for the first time, the lies behind the fairy tales and heroic images our culture feeds on.

RENEWING YOUR MIND

If you're like us, you've probably had moments in your life when you've felt as though some sins will never go away. They are like bad songs playing in your mind, over and over again. You desperately want to break free, but each time you pray, you find yourself stumbling again days, if not hours, later. A lot of times, we don't want to look at what is actually feeding this cycle of sin in our lives.

More often than not, it's the media choices we make. The media **tsunami of seduction** can overtake you in a split second, and if you aren't extremely careful, it can sweep you away and leave you with a long, hard swim back to the safety of the shore.

We know. We've been there.

Most people forget a certain fact about our awesome Savior. Just because he grew up in the first century doesn't mean he wasn't bombarded with sexual pressure. Just because there wasn't MTV in his day doesn't mean his society wasn't dripping with temptation. The Word of God says that we have a high priest (that's Christ) who *empathizes with our weaknesses* (Hebrews 4:15).

> **"FOR WE DO NOT HAVE A HIGH PRIEST WHO IS UNABLE TO EMPATHIZE WITH OUR WEAKNESSES, BUT WE HAVE ONE WHO HAS BEEN TEMPTED IN EVERY WAY, JUST AS WE ARE—YET HE DID NOT SIN." —HEBREWS 4:15**

From a human perspective, mind games seem to be impossible to overcome. But if we look at it from God's eternal perspective, we can clearly see that *every* kind of sin has already been conquered! When Christ bore the weight of our sin on the cross, he took our choices, our guilt, and our shame and physically carried the consequences of our mistakes. By resurrecting as the Savior of the world, Christ paved the way for us to follow him.

Yeah, it's not easy. There are times when our lives are anything but God-honoring, and let's face it: we all make mistakes. But as you continue to grow and change, with the help of the Holy Spirit, the hold sin has on you will become more and more weakened because of the cross of Christ. And you will be able to walk in a greater measure of freedom—freedom from even the kinds of sexual sins that we get tripped up and entangled in: unhealthy relationships, pornography, solo sex, hookups, sexting, and more.

We're talking about freedom from *anything* that holds you back from being more like Christ.

The enemy hates freedom—almost as much as he hates light. Why light? Because light exposes the lies in every heart, mind, and situation. Light enables freedom. The light of God is an extremely powerful tool that allows us to see things as they really are.

"But if we walk in the light, as he is in the light, we have fellow-ship with one another, and the blood of Jesus, his Son, purifies us from all sin" (1 John 1:7).

One way that you can bring light into your life is through accountability. We encourage you to find at least one mentor with whom you can be completely honest about purity, sex, your thought life, what you do when no one is watching, pornography, solo sex—all of it! A mentor is someone of the same sex who is older (usually) and wiser than you, and who can counsel you and advise you in the things of God.

These kinds of relationships will help expose the situation and set you free from being a slave to lust. We encourage you to be accountable to someone who has a higher standard for media than you do. For a time, it might be a good idea to run all of your media intake through your accountability partner. This might sound extreme, but that person can probably give you a different take on what you are watching and listening to and how it is possibly affecting you. This is a small step that you can take to bring your media choices into the light and help you walk in more freedom.

Now that you're moving toward freedom, the next step is to start thinking the way Jesus does! The only way to begin thinking like Jesus is to allow him to renew our minds, day by day. *Our thoughts control our actions*, and this is often more serious than we realize or care to admit.

Why? Because it is unlikely that you will do something that you haven't already thought out in your mind, in one way or another. You're less likely to go make out with that guy at a party if you haven't already thought through what it would be like. You aren't going to have sex with that girl before you're married if you haven't played out the scenario in your head. Our thoughts control our actions—that is why we must make a huge effort to guard them.

OUR THOUGHTS CONTROL OUR ACTIONS.

Hebrews 4:12 says, "The word of God is alive and active. Sharper than any double-edged sword, it penetrates even to dividing soul and spirit, joints and marrow; it judges the thoughts and attitudes of the heart." In order to combat the enemy's lies about lust and to begin renewing your mind, you have to take the Bible at its word. The Bible claims it is sharper than any two-sided sword, so let's start using it as the weapon it is!

SWORD FIGHTING

One of the most beneficial things you can do is memorize Scripture that speaks to your struggles. Here are some examples:

Guys, let's say you're at the mall, and you walk by this store with lingerie ads plastered across the front window. Yeah, it is really tempting to look, but you're committed to keeping yourself pure. *Now* would be a great time to repeat Job 31:1—"I made a covenant with my eyes not to look lustfully at a young woman"—and then book it out of there! Don't hang out around that area—look away and walk away! If you allow those thoughts to dwell and linger, you will stumble, both in the moment and later on that night.

Girls, you're hanging out with a big group of friends on Friday night. After a movie, you're all tired and heading home. The guy you've had a crush on for, like, *ever*, asks if he can drive you home. You are seriously tempted to consider, but also know that, well, you will be seriously tempted. Enter Matthew 6:13: "Lead us not into temptation, but deliver us from the evil one." If you have friends with you, ask for a ride home. If there is no one with you, call a parent or trusted adult to drive you home. It isn't worth putting yourself in a compromising situation just for a convenient drive home with your crush.

Lately your thought life has been slightly less than pure. OK, a lot less. You get to thinking about that guy or girl you really like, and things go way too far in your head. You really want to stop the thoughts from coming, but you've indulged them for so long you aren't sure how to put on the brakes. Memorize Philippians 4:8: "Finally, brothers and sisters, whatever is true, whatever is noble, whatever is right, whatever is pure, whatever is lovely, whatever is admirable—if anything is excellent or praiseworthy—think about such things."

Once you begin memorizing Scripture, it's amazing how quickly it comes to you when you need it. To help you memorize, try putting Bible verses on:

★ **YOUR LOCKER DOOR**

★ **YOUR CELL PHONE SCREEN**

★ **YOUR BEDROOM AND BATHROOM MIRRORS**

★ **YOUR CAR DASHBOARD**

★ **YOUR ALGEBRA BOOK COVER**

★ **THE BILL OF YOUR FAVORITE HAT**

★ **YOUR COMPUTER DESKTOP**

★ **YOUR BEDROOM CEILING**

★ **A PIECE OF PAPER YOU KEEP IN YOUR WALLET**

★ **YOUR KEYCHAIN**

★ **YOUR VOICE MEMO FEATURE ON YOUR CELL PHONE, IF YOU HAVE ONE**

And anywhere else you look all the time!

The Holy Spirit is so eager to help you break free from any hold the enemy may have placed on you through lust—all you have to do is ask for his help! Remember, **with God all things are possible (Matthew 19:26)!** ★

1. How much does media affect your self-image? Think about how you view your body shape, your complexion, the car you drive, the phone you have, the clothes you wear, and the people you hang with. How do you deal with the pressure culture puts on you to "be perfect" or to be someone other than who you really are?

.

2. Have you noticed that many of the things the world tells us we need only leave us temporarily satisfied and always waiting for the next best thing? 1 Timothy 6:6 says, **"But godliness with contentment is great gain."** What did the writer, Paul, mean by "great gain"? What do you think *you* gain by being content?

3. Check out James 4:4. Why do you think you can't be a friend of the world and a friend of God at the same time? Have you ever tried to both fulfill the world's expectation of you and follow God's plan for your life at the same time? How did that work out?

MY JOURNAL

Read Romans 12:1, 2 and 2 Corinthians 10:4, 5. What do these verses tell you about the ability to renew your thinking?

Jot down more thoughts you can use to renew your mind:

QUIZ: WHICH GUY ARE YOU?

1. You're flipping through a magazine at the dentist's office and you can't seem to get your eyes off this one ad, featuring a hottie wearing almost nothing and this chiseled dude looking like he could bench-press Mount Everest. You think:

A. Man, I've got to get myself looking like that guy. If I'm ever going to have a girlfriend, I better get myself to the gym NOW!

B. This is so stupid. Those two don't have anything to do with cologne!

C. I look nothing like that guy and I'll never get a girl like that. I can't stand my body. Whatever.

D. Man, this kind of ad makes so many people stumble. It'd be cool to be built like that guy, but I don't need to be looking at this junk.

2. You and some of the guys go to the movies to see the sequel to that spy flick with that awesome special agent. But now you're feeling like you would be a lot happier if you could have a phone like he does and a laptop and all that other stuff. What do you do?

A. Blow everything you've saved since you started working last year to get that latest iSomething.

B. Go off in anger to the world in your next blog post: "People are so materialistic; it drives me crazy! What about the starving kids in Africa, you selfish idiots?!?"

C. Hang around your house for two days, your head mostly stuck in your computer and video games. Whenever your parents are around, sigh deeply and mutter complaints about how ancient your phone/watch/computer/insert-gadget-here is.

D. Make a decision: all of that stuff is cool, but I don't need it. I'm happy enough as it is. Besides, tomorrow everyone will be crazy over something else, right?

3. Lately you've been watching that teen reality show with all those hotties living the life in the Big Apple. Their morals are, um—OK, they don't have any morals, and their nights are usually filled with hookups and cheap beer. But the more you watch it, the less weird it seems. You're starting to get into it. You think:

A. The first chance I get to live life like that, I'm there. Bible schmible. That God stuff is for, like, my grandparents.

B. Those fools are all going to get an STD and end up dying at about thirty, I just know it. They deserve whatever they get for being so reckless.

C. I would *so* do that if I ever had any friends.

D. I'm not going to waste any more time watching these people destroy themselves. Their choices are going to cause some serious damage later.

So how much does what you see and hear really influence you?

Check out the key on pages 20–21.

QUIZ: WHICH GIRL ARE YOU?

1. You're flipping through a magazine at the dentist's office and you can't seem to get your eyes off this latest and greatest fashion barely covering the body of a stick-thin, gorgeous model. You think:

A. I *so* have to look like that girl. If I'm ever going to get a date with the most popular guy in school, I better start a serious diet.

B. This is *so* stupid. Those clothes don't even look good on her!

C. I look nothing like her. Great. Ugh. I can't stand my body!

D. OMGosh this is so inappropriate. Put some clothes on, people!

2. You and a group of friends go to the movies to see the newest chick flick with that amazingly gorgeous guy and stunning starlet with the equally stunning wardrobe. You start feeling pretty bad about your own life. I mean, where is *your* knight in shining armor, anyway? What do you do?

A. Blow your entire savings account at an incredibly expensive boutique. You send your friend a photo of your favorite new outfit: "Even if I haven't found the love of my life, I'm going to look GOOD while waiting!"

B. Vent to the world in your next blog post: "People are so superficial; it drives me crazy! What about the starving kids in Africa, guys?!?"

C. Mope around your house for two days thinking that you'll always just be stuck with ugly guys and cheap clothes. Whenever your parents are around, sigh deeply and whine about how your clothes are *so* last year.

D. Make a decision: that dream life is cool, but I was happy before, and I'll keep being happy now. And besides, no one ever got the perfect guy because she wore designer heels, right?

3. Lately you've gotten into watching a popular teen reality series featuring beach bums and bathing beauties living the life. Their morals are, um—OK, they don't have any morals, and their nights are usually filled with hookups and cheap beer. But the more you watch it, the less weird it seems. You're starting to get into it. You think:

A. The first chance I get to live life like that, I'm there. Bible schmible. That God stuff is for, like, my grandparents.

B. Those fools are all going to get an STD and end up dying at about thirty, I just know it. They deserve whatever they get for being so reckless.

C. I would *so* do that if I ever had any friends.

D. I'm not going to waste any more time watching these people destroy themselves. Their choices are going to cause some serious damage later.

So how much does what you see and hear really influence you?
Check out the key on pages 20–21.

Mostly As:

There is this super popular belief in our culture today that says you can do whatever you want during your teen years and then live a "Christian" or "serious" life later. But when people blow their youth on booze, partying, and sex, they're crippled (spiritually, mentally, emotionally) when they're finally ready to grow up. A path of self-gratification is a life headed in a dangerous direction; there's just pain and heartache ahead.

You live in the moment, you're the life of the party, someone people love to be around. Don't waste that gift by living for yourself. Use it to point people to Christ . . . there's a good chance they see something in you that they want. Help others to pursue Jesus. Because people like you and want to be around you, that also means that they watch you. You have to be accountable for how others see you. If you can reflect Christ (not the world) in your speech and actions, you will impact people in a big way!

Mostly Bs:

OK . . . our guess is that you're pretty tough. You don't like it when people mess around, screw up, or waste their lives. Those things are good. This conviction will help you in the future to hang onto your faith. However, you're going to have to work to keep a deep sense of compassion and mercy so you're not just "all hammer and no heart."

People want to be told the truth; they know when someone is lying to them. You aren't someone who will sugarcoat the truth or water it down just to stay cool with people. Don't be surprised if people seek you out for advice and answers; you may have that gift. But be sure to always point them to Christ and his Word—you can't do it alone!

Mostly Cs:

When the apostle Paul wrote to his young friend, Timothy, whom he was mentoring, he said, "We brought nothing into the world, and we can take nothing out of it. But if we have food and clothing, we will be content with that" (1 Timothy 6:7, 8). Maybe you've been longing for what the world says you need, and that longing has created a huge hole in your life. How you're living could be showing itself in anger (you can't have what you want—check out James 4:2, 3) or sadness or emptiness (you're missing the whole meaning of life—check out John 10:10).

If God hasn't allowed certain things to come into your life, be thankful! He's probably saving you from a mess of trouble. God's not about to let someone or something take his place in our hearts; he fights for us. Remember: the Bible says that God is a jealous God (Exodus 20:5). He may be taking away distractions so he can take center stage, instead of your own desires. Be encouraged! Get fired up that he has a plan for you! He has your best in mind.

Mostly Ds:

Rock on! It's awesome that you're seeking God and his Word to find answers to life's tough questions. Keep seeking! Keep knocking! Keep asking! He will give you every answer you need and then some (Matthew 7:7-11)! Our guess is that although you may stand out sometimes for being different, you're an unmistakable light to those around you. You aren't moved by the opinion of the crowd or what the popular kids are doing; you find your hope and strength in God.

But remember, always gain your confidence and strength from Jesus, not from yourself. He'll never lead you down the wrong path! "Trust in the LORD with all your heart and lean not on your own understanding; in all your ways submit to him, and he will make your paths straight" (Proverbs 3:5, 6).

A few thoughts from our team:

Remember, no matter what kind of guy or girl you are, God has designed you according to his awesome plan and purpose. These quizzes aren't here to make you feel guilty or stupid; we wrote them to help you see some areas that need adjusting in our lives. So be encouraged, and spend some time and take a solid look at how media affects you. You never know what you might find out!

GUARD THE GATE

IMAGES AND SOUNDS YOU ALLOW INTO YOUR MIND HAVE A TENDENCY TO STICK WITH YOU.

Generations of Virtue has an awesome internship program that runs during the spring and summer of every year, for guys and girls ages seventeen to twenty-one. These youth travel with us all over the U.S., serving and ministering for six intense weeks. One of the rules we have for interns is: "No music from home, cell phones, and/or laptops." Now before you freak out, let us explain.

See, when you're with us on the road, we want you to be able to be totally focused, not thrown off course by your usual distractions. It's a great way to get your attention on the task at hand and let the worries from your hometown drift away for six amazing weeks.

But you don't have to join our internship program to go on a media fast. (Although we'd love to see you there! Check out www.generationsofvirtue.org for more info.) If you're having a hard time keeping your head pure, try taking a media fast on your own, and watch God work!

Images and sounds you allow into your mind have a tendency to stick with you. Our brains were designed to capture and keep information, which is why it's important to guard the gates of our eyes and ears. Did the last movie you saw send images into your mind that you can't seem to shake? The truth is that when we watch a movie or television show, view something online, look at a magazine, or read a book with inappropriate images and scenes, our thoughts dwell on those images.

Are the things you're putting into your mind encouraging you to pursue God? Analyze the fruit of the media you take in and ask yourself a simple question: does this hinder me or does it help me?

On the other side, media can be used as a tremendous influence for good in our lives. Movies and music with strong messages can be vastly helpful; it's all about choosing the right ones. Think of your media intake like a diet. Diets only work with a healthy balance, good proportions, and self-control!

The guys and girls on our team really love to watch movies together, but we're always careful to pick movies that won't cause us to stumble. Two hours of entertainment is not worth searing your brain with permanent, harmful imagery. However, picking out a great movie with a powerful message can start awesome conversations and leave you really thinking!

The same thing is true with music. Music has a way of weaving its way into every aspect of our lives like no other form of media can. Have you ever sat there, enjoying a song, and all of a sudden—BAM!—you actually listen to the words? Often, popular songs have a cool beat but spew out terrible lyrics. And whether we like it or not, those lyrics are going into our minds.

Now, maybe you're sitting there thinking, *Yeah, so what? Who cares about the lyrics? It's not like I'm going to go DO that stuff, I just like the song!* Stick with us a minute. Remember what we just said? Whatever media you allow into your life will directly influence the way you think and the choices that you make.

DOES THIS HINDER ME OR DOES IT HELP ME?

Think about it a sec! All of these musicians, producers, and artists have a message they are trying to convey to you. They sing, write, and record those songs for a reason. Why? Because they want you to buy into their message.

So when you listen to a song, that song goes into your mind. Your mind retains it, because that's what our incredible, God-made minds are designed to do. You may temporarily forget about that song—but it is still recorded in your brain.

Think about what you are listening to, maybe even right now—do you really want *those* lyrics running around in your head all day? If the lyrics that typically circle in your head were projected on a big screen at church, would that make you uncomfortable? If Jesus was sitting there with you, what would he think about it? These are just a few questions to get you thinking. We'll talk about all of this again later. ✶

"Finally, brothers and sisters, whatever is true, whatever is noble, whatever is right, whatever is pure, whatever is lovely, whatever is admirable—if anything is excellent or praiseworthy—think about such things" (Philippians 4:8).

Based on this verse, what ways can you think of to guard the gate? Write about a time you let the enemy past your gate. How can you keep that from happening again? Remember, God will help you in the battle. "He will be a spirit of justice to the one who sits in judgment, a source of strength to those who turn back the battle at the gate" (Isaiah 28:6).

REFLECT/DISCUSS

1. How can you be held accountable for your choices about movies, music, television, and the Internet?

2. What artists, movies, television shows, Internet sites do you need to cut out of your life?

PRACTICE SELF-CONTROL

Recently I (Julie) had a conversation with two teens who believed themselves to be madly in love. At fifteen, they were absolutely positive they had met "the one." While that could be possible (though not probable), I couldn't help but ask what had drawn them so close together. After many discussions the bottom line became clear; their physical relationship was on the slide and headed toward sex.

The desire for intimacy was clouding their ability to make levelheaded choices about one another and the serious direction their relationship was going. Times like this, whether they come at age fifteen, twenty, or twenty-five, must be met with self-control.

By developing self-control now, and continuing to cultivate it as you grow, you are helping yourself to be able to make wise, clear decisions in the future.

Some people seem to think that once they're married, all their desires will be met and there will be no need to deny themselves. But this is far from the truth. Many married people have told us that in several significant ways there is an even greater need to exercise self-control when you're married. That's why we feel it's important to practice self-control *before* marriage.

Self-control is something you learn by denying selfish desires, thoughts, and behaviors. In many ways it is a gift you cultivate to give to your husband or wife. It is a commitment you make that says, "I value you, and I believe our future is more important than my selfish desires."

There are many ways to practice self-control. Ask God to show you ways you can think of others before yourself. **"For the Spirit God gave us does not make us timid, but gives us power, love and self-discipline" (2 Timothy 1:7).**

A lot of opportunities can come up in everyday family life:

★ YOUR SISTER ASKS YOU TO TURN YOUR MUSIC DOWN SO SHE CAN CONCENTRATE; YOU DON'T COMPLAIN OR ARGUE, YOU JUST DO IT.

★ IS THERE ONLY ONE COOKIE LEFT? MAKE SURE YOUR YOUNGER BROTHER GETS IT.

★ WHAT ABOUT HELPING YOUR MOM OR DAD AROUND THE HOUSE?

You may not realize it, but any opportunity you take to help someone else instead of doing what you want to do at that moment is practice in self-control. If you can build up that ability to deny yourself little by little, that tendency will become strong by the time you enter your late teens and twenties.

There are also some very specific mental strategies you can use to practice self-control before you're married. Pretend your future spouse is standing right next to you. If he or she were watching your every move, would you flirt with that person in youth group? How about the movie you watched last night? Are there any scenes in that movie you wouldn't want your future spouse to know you watched? What about the messages you post or the pictures you upload online? Is there anything in those that wouldn't be honoring to your future calling and destiny?

How are your thoughts going? Are you remaining faithful to your future spouse, even in your thought life? In Proverbs 31, we are given an example of a noble wife. In verses 11 and 12 we are told: "Her husband has full confidence in her and lacks nothing of value. She brings him good, not harm, all the days of her life." Guys, you're not exempt! To be able to bring your spouse good all the days of your life, you have to start preparing now.

If you're diligent to practice self-control before you're married, it will help you to be ready for the daily trials and opportunities of being married someday:

★ **THE TIMES YOU DON'T GET YOUR WAY**

★ **WHEN YOUR SPOUSE NEEDS YOUR HELP, LIKE WHEN HE OR SHE IS SICK**

★ **SHARING YOUR LIVING SPACE, BANK ACCOUNT, AND SCHEDULE**

★ **FIGHTING OFF THE TEMPTATION OF INAPPRO- PRIATE RELATIONSHIPS**

If you can learn to be a good servant to the people God has placed in your life now, someday your spouse will receive a very special gift. And even if you don't plan on getting married anytime soon, your practice of self-control will prepare you to be a bold tool of God's will, using the love and power and self-discipline his Spirit gives you.

Galatians 5:19-23 (*The Message*) lays out the differences between living a selfish life and living for God. (Feel free to check out these verses in other Bible versions as well to increase your understanding.) Read it here:

It is obvious what kind of life develops out of trying to get your own way all the time: repetitive, loveless, cheap sex; a stinking accumulation of mental and emotional garbage; frenzied and joyless grabs for happiness; trinket gods; magic-show religion; paranoid loneliness; cutthroat competition; all-consuming-yet-never-satisfied wants; a brutal temper; an impotence to love or be loved; divided homes and divided lives; small-minded and lopsided pursuits; the vicious habit of depersonalizing everyone into a rival; uncontrolled and uncontrollable addictions; ugly parodies of community. I could go on.

This isn't the first time I have warned you, you know. If you use your freedom this way, you will not inherit God's kingdom.

But what happens when we live God's way? He brings gifts into our lives, much the same way that fruit appears in an orchard—things like affection for others, exuberance about life, serenity. We develop a willingness to stick with things, a sense of compassion in the heart, and a conviction that a basic holiness permeates things and people. We find ourselves involved in loyal commitments, not needing to force our way in life, able to marshal and direct our energies wisely.

CHALLENGE

Cool story: Sara, one of the girls on our team, grew up as a total romantic. Movies, books, music—you name it. She loved them all. Problem is, all of that got her really discontent with her own life. Every time she watched one of those movies, listened to one of those songs, or read one of those books, she'd walk away feeling totally down about her own love life.

During a really difficult and lonely time, God started speaking to Sara's heart about fasting. In case you're not familiar with it, fasting is a biblical concept. People who are fasting refrain from certain things (usually food) as a way of drawing closer to God. When we deny ourselves, we are reminded of our moment-by-moment need for him. He often speaks powerfully during those times.

But keep in mind, fasting can be about more than just food; you can fast from other things, too! So Sara made a commitment: she was going to fast from all romantic movies, music, and books for one whole year! And you know what? After that year, when she would watch a cute movie or hear a love song, it didn't bother her! She fasted until the discontentment starved to death.

Was it hard? You bet! Sara had to refrain from a lot of the stuff she would normally do. But God was so faithful to her! He helped her keep her commitment.

Are you having the same problem Sara was? Has your consumption of media left you totally unsatisfied? Try a media fast!

This week we want to challenge you. Take a serious (and possibly painful) eval of your media choices: the music you listen to, websites you visit, TV shows you watch, books you read, games you play—any and all media! What's helping you? What needs to be tossed out? Get rid of anything that is feeding you lies that you've been believing. Clearing out the junk that's been in your way will help you walk in *so* much more freedom!

We all want to be victorious warriors against the enemy. In the Old Testament, you can read about the Israelites and their many battles. (A great read is Joshua chapter 7.) The Israelites could not stand against their enemies until they removed the evil things from among them. If you want a thriving, passionate relationship with the God of the universe, you'll have to do the same! ☆

> **"I JUST WANT TO TELL YOU THAT WE ARE ALL COUNTING ON YOU TO DREAM A DREAM FOR YOUR GENERATION AND FOR YOUR LIFE. THIS IS NOT A POLITE LITTLE INVITATION . . . YOU MUST DREAM!"**
> **—RON LUCE, *RECREATE YOUR WORLD*[1]**

REFLECT/DISCUSS

1. Take a minute and decide: what's your commitment to God regarding media going to be this week? Get together with a friend or accountability partner and share this commitment with them. Why do this? Because by telling someone what you are going to do, it helps hold you accountable.

2. Have you done your evaluation of your media choices yet? Use this space to jot down ideas for a show, song, story, or illustration that you could create to help others understand the message of this session.

These are the things that impacted me the most from "Cinderella Lied, Superman Died":

These are the things I'm still struggling with, that I need to wrestle with in prayer:

PART TWO

BRACE FOR IMPACT

T he media influx that is hitting our generation is incredible. We can't go anywhere or do anything without encountering its constant presence, always tempting us with the greatest gadget or the newest, most impressive technology. Many of us spend more time in virtual reality than we do in our flesh-and-blood world. While this might not seem like a big deal now, it has huge implications for your future.

Life exists in and thrives on real relationships. But how, in this new era, are we supposed to make healthy choices regarding technology and connect with people on a real, relational level?

Parts of this study might be a little uncomfortable. We've found that we're not so good at being subtle, so we're just going to dive right in. Let's get up close and personal. It's the best way for us all to see not just what needs to change, but what can be turned around and used for the glory and kingdom of God. You ready?

RENEWING YOUR MIND

Because of technology, we can go places and do things that even ten years ago we would've thought impossible! We at Generations of Virtue have seen so many good things come about through media and technology. Millions of people have been exposed to the message of Christ through music, blogs, tweets and posts, status updates, satellite TV shows, and virtual churches in online games. Christians are being discipled through podcasts, MP3 resources, and text messaging.

But just like every other good thing, the use of communication devices and technology can be twisted by the enemy. That is why it's vital to be aware of the dangers of porn, trashy music, inappropriate social networking, and explicit or violent shows. The goal for all of us is to help each other not only avoid harmful media but also to use media to advance God's kingdom.

One of the benefits—and disadvantages—of advances in technology is that **everything is right at our fingertips.** It wasn't that many years ago that in order to look at porn or watch an R-rated movie, people had to do so in person. They had to go to an adult bookstore or movie theater—places where age restrictions were enforced. Or they had to walk into a video store and find *that* section—the part where kids were kept from browsing and explicit images were covered up.

But now? Unless someone peeks over your shoulder when you get online or grabs one of your earbuds when you listen to your MP3 player, no one knows what kind of stuff you're consuming. Technology allows us temporarily to ignore this consequence of our sin; it's removed the I-don't-want-to-be-seen-doing-*that* factor.

And yet in all the most important ways, **sin has the same effects it has always had. It has the same rotten fruit.** We can do things in secret and "get away" with them, but that doesn't mean we'll escape all the consequences. Consequences are consequences, and God has designed them for a reason. Those images and lyrics stick in your mind and influence your thoughts long after you first absorb them. Did you know that the repeated act of viewing explicit images can even result in the rewiring of your brain in such a way that you become chemically addicted to the effects? (Craig Gross and Steven Luff, *Pure Eyes*)[2].

Sometimes an unhealthy use of technology doesn't even have to involve sexual content. Maybe you get sucked into trying to get to the next level of a game or watching your four favorite TV shows every night, so you end up spending eight hours a day in front of the TV. While it might seem fun at the time, you have to think—what else could you accomplish in that time? That's a really long time, especially to spend on something as non-eternal as entertainment! If you had eight hours to give to God and God alone, what would *you* do with your time?

The deal is simple: garbage in, garbage out. If we watch bad movies or listen to trashy music on a daily basis, eventually we will go out and try those very same things. Kind of scary, don't you think?

> **"THE EYE IS THE LAMP OF THE BODY. IF YOUR EYES ARE HEALTHY, YOUR WHOLE BODY WILL BE FULL OF LIGHT."**
> **—MATTHEW 6:22**

Here are a few tools we've found to help keep our brains on track:

★ *KEEP A TIME JOURNAL:* TAKE THE NEXT WEEK OR SO AND KEEP A JOURNAL OF HOW YOU SPEND YOUR TIME THROUGHOUT THE DAY. (SEE THE CHART IN THE MAKE IT COUNT SECTION.) DON'T SKIP ANYTHING! IF YOU SPEND FORTY-FIVE MINUTES EATING BREAKFAST—WRITE IT DOWN! AT THE END OF YOUR WEEK, HAVE A MENTOR OR FRIEND REVIEW THE CHART WITH YOU. IF YOU DISCOVER YOU'RE SPENDING TOO MUCH TIME ON SOMETHING THAT ISN'T PROFITABLE, CHANGE IT!

★ *GET AN ACCOUNTABILITY PARTNER:* DEVELOPING A RELATIONSHIP WITH SOMEONE YOU CAN TALK WITH ABOUT YOUR HABITS AND ADDICTIONS IS A CRUCIAL STEP IN THE RIGHT DIRECTION. THERE'S LOTS OF GREAT SOFTWARE OUT THERE THAT WILL LINK YOU TO SOMEONE ELSE, WHO CAN THEN SEE THE PLACES YOU'VE GONE ON THE INTERNET LATELY. (CHECK OUT SOME OF OUR FAVORITES AT WWW.GENERATIONSOF VIRTUE.ORG.) MEET WITH YOUR FRIEND (GUYS WITH GUYS; GIRLS WITH GIRLS) AT LEAST ONCE A WEEK TO TALK ABOUT HOW YOUR STRUGGLE IS GOING. JUST BE SURE TO PICK A PARTNER WHO'S GOING TO HOLD YOU TO A HIGHER STANDARD—NOT A LOWER ONE!

★ *FAST!* OK, SO MAYBE AFTER THIS SESSION YOU'VE IDENTIFIED SOMETHING YOU NEED TO FAST FROM. FASTING IS USEFUL WHEN YOU REALIZE YOU'RE DEPENDING ON SOMETHING TOO MUCH OR YOU'VE DEVELOPED AN UNHEALTHY APPETITE FOR SOMETHING. INSTEAD OF DOING A FOOD FAST, YOU MIGHT CHOOSE TO DO A FACEBOOK FAST OR EVEN AN ONLINE FAST.

★ *THROW IT OUT:* ARE THERE THINGS YOU'RE HANGING ONTO THAT YOU REALLY SHOULD JUST SCRAP? ONE OF OUR TEAM MEMBERS REALIZED THAT SHE WAS FILLING HER MIND WITH MUSIC AND MOVIES THAT WEREN'T HONORING TO GOD. SHE WAS SO CONVICTED SHE THREW AWAY $3,000 WORTH OF DOWNLOADED ENTERTAINMENT— AND SHE FOUND IT WAS WORTH EVERY THROWN-AWAY PENNY. REMEMBER: NO AMOUNT OF MONEY IS WORTH SACRIFICING YOUR MIND FOR!

1. What points from this section stood out the most to you? Why?

2. If you participated in a Culture Shock event skit for "Brace for Impact," which of the skits that you either performed or watched had the most impact for you? Why? How did it speak to you?

3. What do you think about the idea that watching explicit shows can actually affect your brain? Which of the tools to keep your brain on track do you think will be most helpful for you this week?

Read Ecclesiastes 12:14, Luke 8:17, and Psalm 90:8. What do these verses tell us about the things we do "in secret"? Is anything ever really secret?

Jot down some more ideas about how you can keep your brain on the right track:

MAKE IT COUNT

> **"ROLL YOUR WORKS UPON THE LORD [COMMIT AND TRUST THEM WHOLLY TO HIM; HE WILL CAUSE YOUR THOUGHTS TO BECOME AGREEABLE TO HIS WILL . . .]"**
> **—PROVERBS 16:3 (AMP)**

The way you spend your time determines how you live your life. Crazy thought, we know, but it's true! Submit your time to God and see what he does with it.

Open up about your struggles with time-wasting. Bringing all of our secrets into the light is the number-one way to defeat the enemy. Maybe your struggle is with how much time you spend on the Internet. Let's say you spend . . . um . . . three hours every day on social networking sites. When you consider other things you could be doing with that, does that seem a *little* excessive?

We're serious about you keeping a record of how you spend your time, so we've made a table that you can fill in this next week. We know that some things, like getting on the Internet or talking on your cell phone, are necessary for school, work, or life. But we encourage you to be honest and really evaluate how you spend your time on some of these well-known time-wasters.

Use this record for the things you do with technology that are purely for entertainment reasons. However, the last column of this table is for keeping track of how much time you spend doing something super important: praying and reading your Bible.

Journal your time for seven days—then total it all up. It's an eye-opening exercise.

Activity/ Day	Online social networking	Surfing the Web	On the phone	Listening to music/ gaming	Reading magazines	Watching TV/movies	Praying/ reading Bible
Day 1							
Day 2							
Day 3							
Day 4							
Day 5							
Day 6							
Day 7							

After you've kept the chart for a week, come back to it and think about where your time is going. Are you surprised?

We hope this exercise will get you thinking about how to make your time count. How can you use the advantages of technology for furthering the kingdom of God?

Think about your talents. Do you know how to make podcasts and want to spread the gospel (*gospel* means "good news") of Christ or a message that God has placed on your heart? Awesome! Start making them!

Maybe you're a really talented musician. Use recording software to cut an album. Get together with some like-minded performers and make some music—you never know what could come of it.

Or try some of these other ideas:

★ MAKE VIDEO PODCASTS OR DIARIES THAT FOLLOW UP THE MESSAGE YOU HEARD THIS WEEK, OR ON OTHER TOPICS THAT YOU'RE LEARNING ABOUT.

★ VOLUNTEER TO MAKE VIDEO ANNOUNCEMENTS FOR YOUR CONGREGATION.

★ IF YOU HAVE THE TECH SKILL, OFFER YOUR TIME TO MAKE PRESENTATIONS FOR PASTORS OR OTHER SPEAKERS AT YOUR CHURCH.

★ RECORD AN ALBUM FOR YOUR WORSHIP TEAM.

★ BLOG ABOUT WHAT GOD IS SHOWING YOU AND TEACHING YOU THIS WEEK/MONTH.

★ DRAFT SOME TEXT MESSAGES ON SCRIPTURES THAT INSPIRE YOU. TEXT THEM TO FRIENDS THROUGHOUT THE WEEK.

★ IF YOU HAD A GREAT TIME WITH THE SKITS IN THE "BRACE FOR IMPACT" SESSION, WHY NOT KEEP IT GOING? WRITE YOUR OWN PLOTS AND FILM THE SKITS ON YOUR OWN, THEN HAVE A VIEWING PARTY TOGETHER AT YOUTH GROUP. HAND OUT PRIZES FOR THE MOST CREATIVE, BEST OVERALL, AND SO ON. MAKE IT A MINI-OSCARS NIGHT!

. . . And these are only a few ideas that can advance God's kingdom! ☆

1. Read 1 Corinthians 10:31. What are some creative ways you have used or could use technology to advance the kingdom of God? to encourage other believers?

2. How do you feel about the way you use your time? What can you do to remind yourself to make better use of every hour?

What do you dream of doing with your life? How will you make an impact on your world? Brainstorm your ideas and write or sketch about your hopes and dreams here.

GUARD THE GATE

Let's shift gears here a bit and address a heavier technology issue: pornography. Whether you've stumbled onto it accidentally or deliberately sought it out, pornography is an in-your-face issue in our society. Sometimes it seems as if there is no way to escape it.

Well, here's a clue: if you want to avoid it, you have to be intentional. We work with thousands of teens every year, from deep, mentoring relationships to a few hours' acquaintance at events all over the world, and if there's one thing we hear about porn, it's that **addictions most frequently start from *curiosity.***

Maybe this has happened to you, and whether you've developed a habit of looking at porn or not, you *are* affected by it.

Did you know that the pornography industry ("a 57 billion dollar worldwide industry making more than the combined revenues of all the professional football, baseball, and basketball teams in America"[3]) actually targets a very specific demographic? You may be surprised to learn that every day, the people who drive the porn industry are interested in picking off every eight- to twelve-year-old child (girl or boy—it doesn't matter) they can get their hands on.

Why, specifically, do they target this age group? Because they know that at this age children are curious—their brains are developing and they're interested in the world outside their own place in life. And their bodies are developing right alongside their minds. Plus, the people in this industry know that if they can snag a person between the ages of eight and twelve, they'll very likely have a customer for life. It's a critical time in the development of kids, when the brain is forming new connections and exploring thoughts and ideas that were previously closed off. Enter the porn industry—eager to make money and not at all bothered to destroy lives along the way. They don't care if you're male, female, underage, or married—as long as you have money or will have money in the future—they want you.

It's sick, and it's everywhere. But as a youth culture ready to be part of a revolution, we're determined to turn the tide.

Are you trapped in the pit of pornography? We have some practical steps you can take to get your life back on track.

Admit it. Testimony after testimony about someone who has walked away from this lifestyle points out that the person started by admitting the problem to someone. Talk to someone in authority about this issue (your youth pastor, a mentor, your parents, or others). Read James 5:16: "Confess your sins to each other and pray for each other that you may be healed. **The earnest prayer of a righteous person has great power and produces wonderful results**" (*NLT*).

Read up. Choose and read one of the books we've listed at the end of this study. The point is that we all need help, and there is plenty of help if we look for it.

Find an accountability partner ASAP. This battle will most likely be the hardest thing you've ever fought against. Lust is not something to be taken lightly, and once you decide you're going to fight against it, it's going to scream and kick and flail—and try to tear you to pieces. You're going to need someone who is further along in the battle against lust and can honestly hold you accountable to the things you look at, the thoughts you entertain, and the choices you make. Pray about the person you should ask, and ask the Lord to provide exactly who he wants you to be accountable to. This is not a problem you can put off until you get married. That's not the solution. The only way out is to come clean. Remember, you didn't get into porn overnight, and you won't get out of it overnight. This will follow you through your life unless you're intentional about dealing with it now. This is a daily battle to be fought and *won*.

Don't be discouraged if you stumble, because let's face it, we all do. But keep running as fast as you possibly can toward Christ, and he will be faithful to walk you out of this addiction.

Cut off your supply. Get rid of anything you have that's porn-related: bookmarks to sites, saved images, magazines, friendships with the wrong crowd—we're serious when we say *anything*. There are more ways to stumble than you might think. Maybe you need to remove the Internet capabilities from your phone? Whatever has given you access to sexually explicit content has to go. No questions asked.

Watch your influences. Do you have friends you need to confront on the issue of porn or sexual struggles? Don't be afraid to walk away from the friendship if they aren't willing to change. Be sure to convey that you love them, and you really hope they come around to know Jesus and let him set them free. But it's not your job or responsibility to hang around them if they are causing *you* to stumble. Encourage them to find accountability, and then split up until things are settled.

Let's get to the bottom of this thing. What is at the root of the addiction? Where are you not allowing God to fulfill you? Are you looking to something else to satisfy? Do you look to lust to calm you down when you're stressed? hurt? anxious? Is there a pain in your heart you're trying to avoid or at least slow down by turning to pornography? Because **unless you deal with the real heart-issue of what's behind your addiction, it will just pop up again**—in one form or another. Is there someplace you're not allowing the Lord to reach? Pray about this. Know that even if you give up porn, lust, solo sex and anything else that goes with it, if you don't deal with the root issue, it'll just come up somewhere else in your life.

Fight temptation with the sword of the Spirit. Look up Hebrews 4:12. Scripture is truly amazing. It has the power to transform your life one thought at a time. You have thought patterns and images in your mind that you're going to need to erase, and it's not going to be easy. You're going to be tempted to have your mind fixed on those thoughts and images, but this is where the Bible comes in. Scripture is like the scalpel that God uses to perform brain surgery. When you're tempted, work on memorizing Scripture. Keep an index card in your pocket and pull it out whenever the thoughts come. Ask God for relevant Scriptures to help you fight this battle of the mind. Some great verses to start with are:

★ **1 Corinthians 10:13**

★ **1 Corinthians 15:57**

★ **2 Corinthians 10:5**

★ **Job 31:1**

★ **Matthew 5:27-30**

Now, let's say you're *not* curious about porn—that's good! We hope you read this whole section anyway and realize that this issue affects everyone living in our modern-day culture, including you—even if indirectly. Pornography is not just something that captures the person viewing it; it also shapes the way we treat and look at other people. It's promoted terrible things in the treatment of women and children. Being the object of someone's lust leads to being devalued, demeaned, torn apart, and put down. It's just not worth the long-term mental anguish for some short-term excitement. ★

REFLECT/DISCUSS

Note: If you are discussing these questions with others, you should be in a discussion group of the same gender.

1. In what ways do you struggle with keeping your thoughts pure?

2. When do your thoughts tend to stray? Is there a certain time of day or a regular event that triggers lustful thoughts in your head?

3. How does pornography affect the way we look at people, especially those of the opposite sex? Can you see ways that pornography has influenced the way you or others view sexuality? How so?

MY JOURNAL

God created sex, which means it is a good thing. But when we throw in a worldly perspective and take God's gift outside the boundaries he gave us, outside of marriage, his gift becomes a source of havoc in our lives.

If you're reading this study, chances are pretty good that you want to avoid becoming addicted to porn—or if you're already involved, that you want to get out. We strongly suggest that you take a moment to write down a media purity covenant—a list of guidelines and goals about your use of media that you promise to adhere to. You can then post these on your laptop or in your bedroom to help you remember your decision to keep your mind and eyes pure. Here's an example:

> Before God, this day, I choose to keep my eyes, heart, mind, and body pure. I choose to avoid looking at any websites that would compromise my purity, including porn or any other explicit things. I choose to run to Christ and my accountability partner when I am struggling, and by God's grace, I choose to walk in freedom from this addiction.

Share your covenant with your accountability partner as well.

Because porn is so addicting, it often becomes like an idol to us. **(An idol is something that we cling to, trust in, rely on, or put before God.)** Once we decide to get rid of our idols, they can feel like gigantic mountains, like strongholds that are impossible to overcome. But take heart! Remember what the Lord promised Israel in **Jeremiah 31:11** (*NLT*): **"For the Lᴏʀᴅ has redeemed Israel from those too strong for them."** The idol of lust in your heart may feel impossible to break away from, but just like God promised to save Israel, he will save you too. He'll come for your rescue when you cry out to him with all of your heart.

Check out Jeremiah 29:13. What does that verse say to you?

Jonah 2:8 *(The Message)* says: "Those who worship hollow gods, god-frauds, walk away from their only true love." When we trust in idols, when we allow them to take up residence in our hearts, we disrupt the flow of God's Spirit in our lives. We forfeit his supernatural help when we choose idols over him. That's not the position we need to be in if we are going to break free! We absolutely need his help. Take some time to pray and seek the Lord about idols in your life.

Which idols have taken up residence in your heart?

CHALLENGE

This week, find one way that you can use technology to advance God's kingdom. Whether it's making a podcast, creating a blog, or recording an album, find something you can do to further God's kingdom instead of your own agenda.

GREAT READS

Good books we've found that will help in the fight against pornography:

★ **TACTICS, BY FRED STOEKER WITH MIKE YORKEY**

★ **EVERY YOUNG MAN'S BATTLE*, BY STEPHEN ARTERBURN AND FRED STOEKER WITH MIKE YORKEY (*NOTE: WE'VE FOUND THIS BOOK BEST SUITED FOR THOSE WHO HAVE A PROBLEM WITH A PORN ADDICTION AND/OR SEXUAL ADDICTION. IF THIS DOES NOT DESCRIBE YOUR SITUATION, WE RECOMMEND TACTICS OVER THIS ONE.)**

★ **EVERY YOUNG WOMAN'S BATTLE, BY SHANNON ETHRIDGE AND STEPHEN ARTERBURN**

★ **WHAT ARE YOU WAITING FOR?, BY DANNAH GRESH**

MY JOURNAL

These are the things that impacted me the most from this session:

These are the things I'm still struggling with, that I need to wrestle with in prayer:

"GOD IS WAITING FOR YOU. BUT HE IS NOT WAITING BY THE ALTAR, HOPING YOU'LL DROP BY AND TALK FOR A WHILE. HE IS WAITING FOR YOU TO RISE UP AND ENGAGE IN THE BATTLE."
—FRED STOEKER, *EVERY MAN'S BATTLE*[4]

PART THREE

THE POPULARITY CONTEST

For reasons unknown to humankind, at some point or another we all feel it—an all-consuming drive that leads us to do crazy things just to attain it. What is *it*? Popularity.

So what's the problem with that? Well, when our energies and efforts are poured out on winning the popularity contest, we forfeit all the fun and benefit of just being ourselves. We forget who we are. And if there's one thing we at GOV want you to get through this study, it's this—WHO YOU ARE is extraordinary. Your identity is valuable. It's irreplaceable, actually.

RENEWING YOUR MIND

The problem with trying to be the best at everything and constantly competing with each other is that we can't fulfill our own potential, or allow those around us to do so either. Only you can fill the place God has designed for you to fit. If you're busy trying to fill everyone else's role, you won't be able to complete your own purposes.

Romans 8:28 reads: **"And we know that in all things God works for the good of those who love him, who have been called according to his purpose."**

How do you think your talents work together for the kingdom of God? Sometimes we tend to think that God only uses people such as missionaries or pastors to accomplish his work—but that is *far* from the truth. Do you know that God can use you absolutely anywhere? So don't worry about your talent being wasted. Think creatively. If you're willing, you'll be used!

If you focus on your own purpose and destiny and calling, there won't be any time to compare yourself with anyone else or tear each other apart. Remember: Christ is the only person you should be comparing yourself to. Everyone falls short. We're all here to become more like Christ, not more like each other!

The Bible doesn't say, "You were put on this earth to be more like Tim from your algebra class." NO! It says, "For God knew his people in advance, and he chose them to become like his Son, so that his Son would be the firstborn among many brothers and sisters" (Romans 8:29, *NLT*).

Jesus Christ is our example. There is no need to look around and compare.

A story from our team:

Hi guys, this is Kate Lockhart and Kelsey Roberts from the GOV team. We wanted to share with you a story about our friendship and what God brought us through. We're great friends now, but you never would've thought so if you'd seen us a while ago! Then it was a very different story. It was a chilly autumn season in upstate New York . . .

We were in high school when our families met through mutual friends. We instantly realized the similarities in one another—in appearance, personality, clothes, and social circles. We were both used to having our own way and did not appreciate it when anyone (and we mean *anyone*) interfered with it. When I (Kelsey) realized that Kate was a challenge to my "Queen Bee" throne, things got ugly. We were definitely acting out from a strong sinful nature. We started gossiping about one another, fighting, and spreading rumors about each other, even to our pastors and parents.

Eventually, the issue was confronted face-to-face by our loving parents and mentors by bringing our behavior out into the light. These wise authorities explained to us that we were operating from a mind-set of trying to be "the best" or "the one."

Kelsey and I (Kate) decided that we really did want to be close and have an **"iron sharpens iron"** (Proverbs 27:17) kind of friendship. We started serving together (super important!) and hanging out more, and as things came up, Kelsey and I would talk things through. We had truthful conversations with one another ("I can't stand you!" and "Why did you do that?"). At the end of the day, we were determined to be friends.

We are GREAT friends today because we were able to ditch the attitude and not step on each other to get to the top. Remember: refuse to get offended! Don't get hurt by your friends telling you the truth about yourself. If they are good friends, and if they're brave enough to say it to your face—then listen up.

REFLECT/DISCUSS

1. Are you ever tempted to compare yourself with those around you? If you're at all honest, you'll probably say yes. List some reasons why that's not a great idea.

2. How do you decide who your close friends are? Is it just based on how well you get along, or does it go deeper than that? Talk about how you make those decisions.

3. What if one of your good friends told you something about yourself that you didn't want to hear? Would you be up for listening or would you ditch the friendship? What would help you choose the first option and not the second?

**"Then you will know the truth, and the truth will set you free"
(John 8:32).**

When Jesus spoke these words, he was referring to the truth of who he is and the light
he brings. As children of God, we can take this verse and apply it to the truth about
ourselves. When we can know the truth about who we truly are (the good, the bad, and
the ugly), then we will be able to work through the things that are not pleasing to God.
Think of it like this: if the Lord were to take a flashlight and shine it into your heart, what
would he see?

Take a moment to write your thoughts here.

IN THE ZONE

Choose True or False for each of the questions in the five zones below. When you're done with each zone, count your true answers, then count your false answers, and add them up below each zone. Check out the results after the quiz to see where you're at, and below each zone result is a passage of Scripture that will help you rise above and change the way you treat those around you.

You should know: there are no right or wrong answers to this quiz! This is merely used as a light to show you where you might be tempted to engage in the popularity contest so that you can be more useful to team efforts in the kingdom of God. So let's get started!

ZONE 1

True or False: I know that God wants me to love people. So I'm pretty cool with my friends—I think that counts.

True or False: As long as I'm a "good" Christian, I'll get to Heaven.

True or False: Gossiping really isn't that big of a deal. As long as I'm nice to people to their faces, I don't see what the problem is.

Total True:_____ **Total False:**_____

ZONE 2

True or False: What I want is my biggest drive in life, and I go after it, especially with my friends.

True or False: I really don't like it when people mess up my plans, and if I don't get my way, I get ticked.

True or False: When it comes to my friends, I tend to be an influencer instead of being influenced, and I can usually get what I want from them.

Total True:_____ **Total False:**_____

ZONE 3

True or False: I love looking good, and I always surround myself with people who make me look good.

True or False: I think people should always pay attention to me. I like being center stage.

True or False: Being rejected is the WORST thing in the world to me. If people don't notice me, I'm totally humiliated.

Total True:_____**Total False:**_____

ZONE 4

True or False: If I don't like a situation, I mentally check out.

True or False: I use things like TV, movies, video games, shopping, social media, porn, or other things like these to help me forget my problems.

True or False: I usually get caught up in daydreams or fantasies about what my life should look like, or could look like in the future.

Total True:_____**Total False:**_____

ZONE 5

True or False: I like the idea that my life is my own, and I can make my own choices.

True or False: I don't usually like people (especially authority figures) telling me what to do.

True or False: The idea that all of my choices or actions are subject to God is uncomfortable to me. I don't like the idea of me or my friends having to answer to anyone, and don't see why we should have to.

Total True:_____**Total False:**_____

If you answered True to two or more in Zone 1 . . .

Law Enforcer: Sometimes you get caught up believing that what you do is more important than who you are. The truth is that God cares way more about who you are on the inside than who you pretend to be on the outside. He isn't interested in your faking nice or pretending to be a good friend—he wants genuine love from his kids.

So next time you're tempted to just *act* like a friend instead of really being a true friend, think again. Make it a point to stop rumors cold when they start spreading around to you. Always assume the best of people instead of the worst, and when people start talking smack, defend the person who's being trashed. It takes someone with a huge dose of character to do that, but we promise—it's worth it. You're a strong person, so use that strength to go after the Word of God, not your own agenda.

WHAT'S THE WORD?

"These are the words of the Amen, the faithful and true witness, the ruler of God's creation. I know your deeds, that you are neither cold nor hot. I wish you were either one or the other! So, because you are lukewarm—neither hot nor cold—I am about to spit you out of my mouth. You say, 'I am rich; I have acquired wealth and do not need a thing.' But you do not realize that you are wretched, pitiful, poor, blind and naked. I counsel you to buy from me gold refined in the fire, so you can become rich; and white clothes to wear, so you can cover your shameful nakedness; and salve to put on your eyes, so you can see" (Revelation 3:14-18).

If you answered True to two or more in Zone 2 . . .

Smooth Operator: You tend to think that what you want is the most important thing in the world, and you're an influencer for sure! When it comes to your friends, you know how to get your way. The downside to this is that people perceive you as being pushy or demanding because they don't feel like what they want or need is important to you at all—probably because you never let them have an opinion.

Next time you're in a situation where you'd normally demand your own way, take a step back. See what those around you think or want to do. You may be surprised at what you hear. Now here's the good news: you're a natural leader, which is awesome! But the greatest leaders on earth are those who are first and foremost servants, and are always willing to listen and take input. Remember to keep yourself submitted to authority, and watch the Lord richly bless your life!

WHAT'S THE WORD?

"And he died for all, that those who live should no longer live for themselves but for him who died for them and was raised again. So from now on we regard no one from a worldly point of view. Though we once regarded Christ in this way, we do so no longer. Therefore, if anyone is in Christ, the new creation has come: The old has gone, the new is here!" (2 Corinthians 5:15-17).

If you answered True to two or more in Zone 3 . . .

The Star Performer: You love being the center of attention. Whether you're at school, a party, or at church or youth group—you feel the need to be front and center. Drama and rumors probably surround you pretty often, because you don't mind speaking your mind or making a scene. The problem with taking the spotlight is that it doesn't leave room for anyone else to shine. It's hard to be happy for other people—even your friends—when they get attention, because you really want it for yourself. Your frustration with that can lead you to put them down out of your anger, when it really has nothing to do with that person—it has everything to do with your being jealous.

Next time you're not center stage—and it's a good idea to make it a POINT to pull yourself out of the limelight from time to time—really pray and ask God to help you be happy for the person who *is* getting the attention. You'll see a whole different perspective on life when you aren't blinded by the bright lights of stardom. Since you're talkative and outgoing, people will tend to feel comfortable with you, so jump at the opportunity to love and listen to others!

WHAT'S THE WORD?

"Then James and John, the sons of Zebedee, came to him. 'Teacher,' they said, 'we want you to do for us whatever we ask.' 'What do you want me to do for you?' he asked. They replied, 'Let one of us sit at your right and the other at your left in your glory.' 'You don't know what you are asking,' Jesus said. 'Can you drink the cup I drink or be baptized with the baptism I am baptized with?' 'We can,' they answered. Jesus said to them, 'You will drink the cup I drink and be baptized with the baptism I am baptized with, but to sit at my right or left is not for me to grant. These places belong to those for whom they have been prepared.' When the ten heard about this, they became indignant with James and John. Jesus called them together and said, 'You know that those who are regarded as rulers of the Gentiles lord it over them, and their high officials exercise authority over them. Not so with you. Instead, whoever wants to become great among you must be your servant, and whoever wants to be first must be slave of all'" (Mark 10:35-44).

If you answered True to two or more in Zone 4 . . .

The Escape Artist: Your life's motto could be "When the going gets tough, I leave." You don't like it when things are difficult or uncomfortable. The easiest way for you to avoid reality is to mentally check out—playing video games, watching a ton of TV or movies, viewing porn, shopping all day long, always talking on the phone . . . or anything else you can do to forget about what is really going on.

You might not realize you are doing this at all. Over the next week, work hard to recognize this habit. Whenever something comes up that's hard for you to deal with, try running to your Bible instead of to the remote control or your phone. Remember: Christ is our strength and provider and best friend. You'll be amazed at the results. Our guess is that you probably have a really compassionate heart, and that is part of the reason why it's difficult for you to look at reality, because sometimes reality hurts. Badly. But know that the Lord holds all things in his hands; don't be discouraged when you see hard things in your life. Be moved to pray for those around you who need help and hope.

WHAT'S THE WORD?

"But you, *keep your head in all situations, endure hardship,* do the work of an evangelist, discharge all the duties of your ministry. For I am already being poured out like a drink offering, and the time for my departure is near. I have fought the good fight, I have finished the race, I have kept the faith. Now there is in store for me the crown of righteousness, which the Lord, the righteous Judge, will award to me on that day—and not only to me, but also to all who have longed for his appearing" (2 Timothy 4:5-8, emphasis ours).

If you answered True to two or more in Zone 5 . . .

The Rebel: You like calling the shots in your life. When you go and hang out with your friends, you want to do *what* you want, *when* you want to do it. If anyone crosses you and tries to interfere with your plans, you get ticked and tend to hold a grudge. In fact, we're guessing that you're not a huge fan of us for saying this to you now. But here's the deal: authority was created by God, and it's super important to stay under the people that God has placed in your life to lead you. You don't want to run out from under that protection—we promise, you'll regret it later if you do.

Next time you're hanging out with your friends, try to stay where you'll be accountable to someone older and wiser than you. It'll save you a world of heartache in the future. You're brave and not afraid to take chances. Never lose that edge; you'll need it when God calls you to do tough things, things that go against the status quo and popular opinion. Just realize that you need people watching over you to keep you in check. OK? We all do.

WHAT'S THE WORD?

"Let everyone be subject to the governing authorities, for there is no authority except that which God has established. The authorities that exist have been established by God. Consequently, whoever rebels against the authority is rebelling against what God has instituted, and those who do so will bring judgment on themselves. For rulers hold no terror for those who do right, but for those who do wrong. Do you want to be free from fear of the one in authority? Then do what is right and you will be commended. For the one in authority is God's servant for your good. But if you do wrong, be afraid, for rulers do not bear the sword for no reason. They are God's servants, agents of wrath to bring punishment on the wrongdoer. Therefore, it is necessary to submit to the authorities, not only because of possible punishment but also as a matter of conscience" (Romans 13:1-5).

Thoughts from the team:

You probably answered "True" in more than one zone. Think about where all of these insights apply in your life. For us, this exercise has been hugely helpful in taking a good look at ourselves and working out how we can become better friends—and more like Christ.

GUARD THE GATE

Sometimes in this whole popularity thing we get so caught up in fitting in or standing out that we forget why in the world we're trying to impress each other anyway. The truth is, most of our reasons for chasing after approval stem from . . . fear. Our goal with this study is to help you guard against any form or kind of fear. Fear can grow into hurt, insecurity, or jealousy—feelings that lead us to engage further in the popularity contest.

Since most of our team is of your generation, we're going to write like you're sitting with us in this big living room at our weekly Bible study, maybe downing your second Dr Pepper of the night. If you were sitting here, we'd ask you point-blank: Do you feel the need to one-up each other all of the time? Why is being the best such a huge drive for all of us? What's the deal?

The Generations of Virtue team is close—we eat together, a lot of us room together, and we travel together 24/7/365. We've had to go through fire together. We've had to hash out a lot of issues about getting along and giving up our desire to be the best.

During the really rough times, our mentors would pull us aside and help us walk through these issues. The advice they gave was incredible. It went something like this: "The feeling of jealousy that you have toward one another only comes from fear of loss." When we all looked at them like, "Huh?" they continued. "Whether it's this huge fear of losing your position or losing who you've built yourself up to be, it all comes from the same thing."

Are you afraid of losing the position of "most popular" in your clique? Or maybe you're afraid of:

- ★ **NOT BEING FAVORED BY YOUR TEACHERS**

- ★ **YOUR COACH NOT PUTTING YOU IN TO PLAY**

- ★ **NOT GETTING THE PART YOU WANTED IN THE SCHOOL PERFORMANCE**

- ★ **THE NEW KID COMING IN AND TAKING YOUR PLACE IN THE WORSHIP BAND**

- ★ **NOT BEING VALEDICTORIAN WHEN YOU GRADUATE**

- ★ **. . . OR COUNTLESS OTHER THINGS**

We have to understand that *nothing good is lost in God*. (Go back and look at Romans 8:28.) Often we're so concerned about maintaining our status—whether it's with our friends, in our families, or in our churches—that we forfeit our own calling in pursuit of someone else's. We get so caught up in wanting what everyone else has that we never develop who we are in Christ or what God gave us (individually) as his children.

Nothing that comes from him can be lost in him. We don't have to worry about someone coming in and trying to knock us out of our place before God. If we're in God's will, nothing can shake that position. Nothing can shake who we are in Christ. God alone will secure our place. We don't have to hold it all together; when we walk with him, he handles that for us.

If you can accept that God gave you incredible gifts and talents, while he also gave those around you different incredible gifts, you can give up wanting *everything* and be content and satisfied with what God gave you. No one gets everything. If we are *supposed* to have something, God will make sure we get it! We all get a part and that part is meant to be shared and combined with those around us to create a massive body—the body of Christ. (Check out pretty much the entire chapter of 1 Corinthians 12!)

See, God is so good that he doesn't show partiality to his kids (Romans 2:11), so we can actually be happy for people when they get something that maybe we wish we had. Did you know that true broth-

> **"GOD DOES NOT SHOW FAVORITISM." —ROMANS 2:11**

erly love is taking the same satisfaction in someone else getting awesome things as if it were happening to you? Wow! That is a huge challenge. But we really believe that if we give up our mind-set that we have to have everything—and that we deserve everything— we'll be able to function as we were designed to, with love and respect for one another.

Do you ever think about what is going on when we are jealous or gossip or backstab? When we reject someone or put a person down, we are actually saying, "I'm afraid of you. You are a threat to me, and I don't like it." Kind of puts things into perspective, doesn't it? When we do those things to people, we can cause them to question who they are—or who they could be—in Christ, just because we don't *feel* like dealing with our fear.

The truth is that forfeiting someone else's well-being for the sake of jealousy is a disgusting transaction. We all know it happens. And we all know it has to stop.

When you have true confidence in Christ and who he has made you to be, there is no fear of things falling apart or losing who you are in him. You can't un-become who you are in Christ. There is so much safety when we operate from a place of humility instead of from the kingdom we seek to create for ourselves. Next time you're tempted to put someone down, trace your thoughts. Why do you want to do that? What's in it for you? What's your drive for doing it?

You may come up with some interesting conclusions.

1. **Check out Proverbs 18:24: "One who has unreliable friends soon comes to ruin, but there is a friend who sticks closer than a brother."** Let's take a look at that first phrase: "One who has unreliable friends soon comes to ruin." What does that say to you?

2. Let's go a little deeper. Do you hang close to your friends? How do you support them? Think about a time when a friend relied on you for help. What happened? Did you come through for that person or not? If you could go back and change that experience, how would you change it?

3. Having as many friends as you possibly can may seem like it's the most important thing right now, because sometimes it looks like the popular kids can do whatever they want. They call the shots, they get the hot dates, they get everyone's attention—but that's all surface. If we're reading what the Word of God says—"One who has unreliable friends soon comes to ruin"—then we have to take a different look at our motives in pursuing popularity.

Let's jump to the second half of the verse: "but there is a friend who sticks closer than a brother." What's so incredible about Jesus is, he is *always* that friend to us. He is there for us through anything, and he longs to be close to us! People will always let us down. No matter how hard they try, they will fall short. But Christ will never leave us or let us down. How does knowing that change the way you look at yourself? at others?

4. Next let's go over to Proverbs 13:20: "Walk with the wise and become wise, for a companion of fools suffers harm." Take an honest evaluation of the people you spend your time with. Are they the type of people who are encouraging you toward God, or are they drawing you away from him? How can you tell? Hint: **1 Corinthians 15:33** tells us that **"Bad company corrupts good character."**

That's not to say that you and your friends have to always be doing "holy" things together. No one expects you to spend every Saturday night in a prayer meeting or to fast together every week (although those are awesome things to do!). Just ask yourself an honest question: are you more or less like Christ when you're around your friends? Why? Write about your feelings and your reactions here.

5. **Proverbs 27:17** gives an important insight about friendship: **"As iron sharpens iron, so one person sharpens another."** If you have ever watched a knife or scissors being sharpened, you know that it involves slashing two pieces of hard, tough metal against each other to make the cutting edge sharper, to make it more useful. When this writer compared us to "iron sharpening iron," what do you think he meant by that?

We often view friendship as a relationship that makes us feel or look good. When we do this, we don't view it the way God intended. While friendships can be awesome, they also serve as a shaping instrument in our lives. A real friend is willing to say—with love—"That wasn't cool that you lied to your parents about where you were last night" or "Hey, I know you really like that girl, but she isn't following after God, and I don't want to see you stumble."

That might seem really hard to do, but that's what friends *should* do! Real friends help each other out, stick with each other, and commit to grow together as brothers and sisters in Christ. They sharpen one another to help each other become more and more like Christ every day.

Take a minute to reflect: Are you willing to be sharpened? Who does that for you now? How would you react if your close friend called you out on something?

6. One of Jesus' most impactful statements is found in **John 15:13.** Jesus told his disciples, his closest friends on earth, **"Greater love has no one than this: to lay down one's life for one's friends."**

Now, most of us won't be put into a life-threatening situation where we physically have to die in order to save a friend's life. So what does Jesus mean when he says to "lay down one's life"? He means to sacrifice yourself for the sake of your friends. He means to put aside what we want and accept what Christ has called us to do. Are you willing to lay down your life for your friends? In what ways can you do this? Take a minute to brainstorm ways you can help those around you:

7. Ecclesiastes 4:9, 10 tells us, **"Two are better than one, because they have a good return for their labor: If either of them falls down, one can help the other up. But pity anyone who falls and has no one to help them up."** Have you ever experienced a friend helping you up when you have fallen—basically, when you've totally messed up? How did it change the outcome of the situation for you? Are you willing to be the type of person who sticks with your friend, even when he or she messes up—and even if it's big-time? What can you do to be ready to catch your friends when they fall?

8. What does the world most often tell you about how your friends are supposed to act or what friends do for each other? Think of movies you've seen, music you've heard, things you've read online. Do you think these viewpoints portray God's view of friendship? Why or why not? Based on what we've talked about, what do you think God expects from friendship? Think of at least three things.

"For as you well know, we never resorted either to words of flattery or to any cloak to conceal greedy motives or pretexts for gain, as God is our witness" (1 Thessalonians 2:5, *AMP*).

Nothing is more shallow than to pretend to be nice to someone when you're really boiling with jealousy. We've felt this before—a tendency to flatter our rivals with words we don't really mean—but it doesn't ever get us anywhere in the end. Instead of saying something you don't mean, really pray and ask God to make you genuinely happy for the person. You could even take a minute to write a prayer on his behalf. Specifically ask God to bless the person and his life. Read **1 Thessalonians 5:11: "Therefore encourage one another and build each other up, just as in fact you are doing."**

The Word tells us over and over again: Dude, help each other out! (OK, different wording, but you get the idea.) The Bible doesn't say, "Don't worry about everyone else, just help your friends out" or "You only have to help the people you like." Nope. It says everyone. Look at **Luke 6:30: "Give to everyone who asks you, and if anyone takes what belongs to you, do not demand it back."**

What are some habits that you need to change to treat everyone (not just certain people) the way that God wants you to?

Jot down some ways you can be more helpful to those around you. It doesn't have to be something huge; it can be a small thing. Just go for it!

CHALLENGE

OK, here goes. Deep breath. Check out these challenges we've got for you.

1. For one week, we want you not to talk negatively about anyone. At all. This includes in your thoughts! Your week's mantra is: "If I don't have anything nice to say (or think!), I won't say (or think!) anything at all." See? Kindergarten does teach us something!

2. Find at least one person you're typically not friends with—or even someone you don't like—and show them the love of Christ. That person may have never heard about Jesus. Maybe they aren't as blessed as you are. You may be the first person to ever show or tell them, "Hey. You're loved." Go ahead. Invite them to church or to hang out with you and your friends this weekend. You never know, it may be your only shot to reach out to them. Remember this: Love isn't a feeling. It's a choice we make to rise above our situation and care for one another no matter what.

3. Instead of the typical smear campaign that some teens engage in, launch a clean campaign. Make it a point to text at least three people encouraging (biblical) messages every day for a week. Don't say anything fake (remember, we're not into false flattery!); be genuine. You'll ruin your witness as a Christian if you are fake with people—try hard to keep it real.

4. It is so important that you understand who you are in Christ. If you can understand this, you won't fall to the lies of the enemy that feed jealousy and anger. There are a ton of Scriptures on this topic, and we encourage you to post these everywhere. All over your room, your bathroom mirror, your car, your locker—anywhere you look all the time! Here are some verses for you to check out:

★ JOHN 1:12; 15:5, 15, 16

★ ROMANS 5:1, 2; 8:1, 2, 28, 31-39

★ 1 CORINTHIANS 3:16; 6:17-20; 12:27

★ 2 CORINTHIANS 1:21, 22; 5:17-21

★ EPHESIANS 1:3-8; 2:6-10; 3:12

★ PHILIPPIANS 1:6; 3:20; 4:13

★ **Colossians 1:13, 14; 2:9, 10; 3:1-4**   ★ **Hebrews 4:14-16**

★ **2 Timothy 1:7**   ★ **1 John 5:18**

From the team:

Hey, remember that we're praying for you! All of this changing is a huge step in the right direction. The Bible says that unity is critical. These small steps will help you navigate out of enemy territory, which is filled with selfishness, and into the kingdom of God, where it's all about loving and serving Christ and each another.

MY JOURNAL

These are the things that impacted me the most from this session:

These are the things I'm still struggling with, that I need to wrestle with in prayer:

79 ☆ THE POPULARITY CONTEST

"I CANNOT GIVE YOU THE FORMULA FOR SUCCESS, BUT I CAN GIVE YOU THE FORMULA FOR FAILURE, WHICH IS: TRY TO PLEASE EVERYBODY."
—HERBERT B. SWOPE[5]

PART FOUR

FEARLESS PURITY

O ur team *loves* love. We aren't here to be down on romance or sex—we're actually all for it! But there's a catch. For centuries misguided relationships have broken the hearts of countless men and women—and all pretty much for the same reason. The people in these failed relationships all tried to have it their own way, not going to Jesus for guidance, but choosing to navigate this territory alone. The Bible says that **"people look at the outward appearance, but the LORD looks at the heart" (1 Samuel 16:7)**. Removing God from the picture is sure to send us down a road of heartbreak. And ultimately, no one wants that—not you, not us, no one.

Will you join us in our pursuit of awesome, successful, God-centered relationships?

RENEWING YOUR MIND

Our ministry has spent significant amounts of time in Southeast Asia. On one particular trip, Bangkok, Thailand, was on our itinerary. Now, Bangkok is known throughout the world as a sort of sexual fantasyland. To many, it's seen as "the pinnacle"—sex at its most mysterious and greatest. Even as our plane made its descent, the overhead speaker was loudly blaring sexually explicit music. Not knowing what to expect, except for what we'd heard in rumors, we set out for our meetings—blithely unaware of what the real Bangkok is like in some places.

Our first surprise was the filth. The odor of vomit, trash, urine, and smoke seemed to permeate everything. From the food stands to the faces of the disabled children begging in the streets (while their parents watched from the alley shadows) to the walls of the buildings, filth was everywhere.

Our meetings took us to one of the most notorious streets in the city, in the heart of the red-light district. As we continued to our destination, our team became more and more disgusted. We found it strange that, when we arrived, the area was nearly deserted. Signs that looked like they'd been salvaged from the ruins of a 1940s-era men's club and featuring phrases like "girls, girls, girls" were crookedly hanging from second-story windows. Our disgust grew as we were called out to by madams, carefully guarding their brothel doorways. We thought: *Can you believe this is a tourist hot spot?*

If you're wondering how thousands of visitors can overlook the sickening exteriors, we'll give you a hint: they only go at night. At dusk hundreds of street vendors appear, many more food stalls are put up, and a crowd begins to gather. Before long the bars and brothels open and the area becomes alive with activity. The filth is so covered up by darkness and cheap merchandise that almost no one, except the locals, ever sees what we saw. Is this what the world does? Covers up its filth and sick ideas with enough darkness and distractions that we can't see what it is we're actually doing?

We share this story with you because, for our team, it served as an awakening. If this is the pinnacle of what the world has to offer, there must be something better. We had to have been created for more than a series of one-night stands, sexual addictions (including pornography), STDs, and emotional heartbreak.

So it's become the quest of our team to find out what God's idea of love really is. We see clearly what the world offers; what does God have for us? God, who created love and sex to begin with. God, who orchestrated the most amazing love stories in history.

We don't hear often enough about God's plan for love and sex. It's not usually part of the plots of best-selling movies, TV shows, or novels. The enemy, the great deceiver and impersonator, has taken what God created for good and manipulated and distorted it into something so perverted from its original purpose that it's almost completely unrecognizable. And to add to his perversion, he tells us this is the best there is.

We believe that God wants to change our thinking when it comes to sex and relationships. How awesome could this be: to be part of a generation of people who are emotionally whole; living out their callings in God; having happy marriages; and having great, healthy, beautiful, fearless sex?

When we bypass what the world offers, forsaking the message that we are subject to the whims of our passions and urges, that life is totally possible.

REFLECT/DISCUSS

1. In what ways have you seen filth (immoral or ungodly behavior, attitudes, or actions) covered up by darkness or distractions? (For example: people use humor to cover up filth in dirty jokes.)

2. Have you ever stopped to think that God is the real creator of sex? That the enemy isn't the creator, so he couldn't possibly come up with anything better than God? Talk or write about what that means, that *God* himself is the creator of sex. What does that mean to you? to your future?

3. If you believe that there's something better for you than the world's view of sex, what influences in your life need to change? TV? Movies? Music? Get specific.

What the Bible says about sexual purity:

★ "For God will bring every deed into judgment, including *every hidden thing*, whether it is good or evil" (Ecclesiastes 12:14, emphasis added).

★ "You have heard that it was said, 'You shall not commit adultery.' But I tell you that anyone who looks at a woman lustfully has already committed adultery with her in his heart" (Matthew 5:27, 28).

★ "What comes out of a person is what defiles them. For it is from within, out of a person's heart, that evil thoughts come—sexual immorality, theft, murder, adultery, greed, malice, deceit, lewdness, envy, slander, arrogance and folly" (Mark 7:20-22).

★ "But among you there must not be even a hint of sexual immorality, or of any kind of impurity, or of greed, because these are improper for God's holy people" (Ephesians 5:3).

★ "Flee the evil desires of youth and pursue righteousness, faith, love and peace, along with those who call on the Lord out of a pure heart" (2 Timothy 2:22).

★ "For you have spent enough time in the past doing what pagans choose to do—living in debauchery, lust, drunkenness, orgies, carousing and detestable idolatry" (1 Peter 4:3).

These verses are hard to argue with. Obviously, God cares a lot about sexual purity! And if he takes the time to warn us again and again throughout the Bible to live sexually pure lives, we should take the time to pay attention to the warnings.

Few people will disagree with certain verses in the Bible, such as "You shall not kill" and "Love your neighbor." But when you start mentioning verses like the ones above (if anyone knows them at all), everyone gets quiet. Why is that?

If we are honest with ourselves, we have to admit that at some point or another we've watered down our standards to reflect those of society. We would never argue our right to murder someone or discuss how hating our neighbors a little bit is OK. Why don't we take these verses about sexual purity as seriously? There's no way we can justify or defend sleeping around, having sexual encounters outside of marriage, or looking at porn.

MY JOURNAL

"Blessed are the pure in heart, for they will see God" (Matthew 5:8).

Do you think this statement from Jesus includes sexual purity? We often fall into a distorted way of thinking: we can stubbornly hold onto our bad habits, still have a relationship with God, and he won't really care what we do. Can you see how the choices you make in relationships and sex directly affect your relationship with God? Journal your thoughts here.

A LITTLE IMAGINATION

Imagine for a moment that as you're walking out of the mall this Saturday, you run into your pastor, who has with him a little boy you've never met. Come to find out, the boy is eight years old, orphaned, and living with an uncle who couldn't care less about his welfare. A strong sense of compassion comes over you, and before you know it, you're joining your pastor in an effort to check up on this kid every day after school.

Describe the different ways you might help him.

Flash forward ten years. By now you've invested a lot of time, energy, and even money in this kid! You've helped him out every way you knew, and most recently, you helped him get into a good college.

The first weekend available, you take off and visit your freshman friend. You're alarmed when you find his dorm room deserted, except for his stoned roommate. After a two-day search involving police, you finally track him down. Sleeping in an alley two blocks from a homeless shelter, he tells you he's decided to live on the streets instead of going to school.

What would you say to him? How would you feel?

Obviously, you'd be hurting badly for your friend. How could he give up all the support and potential he has to live a life on the streets?

But are we any different? We do exactly the same thing when we choose our own path in the world of relationships. How do you think Jesus must feel when we throw away his support and all the promise we have in him, and choose something so far below what he wants for us?

You may be wondering, *What* does *he want for me?*

★ **"THE THIEF COMES ONLY TO STEAL AND KILL AND DESTROY; I HAVE COME THAT THEY MAY HAVE LIFE, AND HAVE IT TO THE FULL" (JOHN 10:10).**

★ **"AND I PRAY THAT YOU, BEING ROOTED AND ESTABLISHED IN LOVE, MAY HAVE POWER, TOGETHER WITH ALL THE LORD'S HOLY PEOPLE, TO GRASP HOW WIDE AND LONG AND HIGH AND DEEP IS THE LOVE OF CHRIST, AND TO KNOW THIS LOVE THAT SURPASSES KNOWL-EDGE—THAT YOU MAY BE FILLED TO THE MEASURE OF ALL THE FULLNESS OF GOD" (EPHESIANS 3:17-19).**

Life to the full. Filled to the measure of all the fullness of God. Having a love that surpasses knowledge. These are the things God wants for us. Whether we ever get married or not, he wants us to know the life and the love that he has designed just for us. Read the Scriptures. Study all the promises God makes to his people. (It will take a while!) This is what he doesn't want us to give up.

But what if you *do* long for a partner in your life? In his letter to the Corinthians, Paul tells them this: **"The wife does not have authority over her own body but yields it to her husband. In the same way, the husband does not have authority over his own body but yields it to his wife"** **(1 Corinthians 7:4).** Your body is not your own. It belongs first to God and then, someday, it will be given to your spouse. What kind of person do you want to have authority over your body? What kind of body do you want to give that person?

Picture your dream husband or wife. There they stand, so perfect you can hardly believe it. They look exactly like what you have always wanted. Now imagine you find out that your perfect person is addicted to porn, solo sex, casual sex, drugs, or drinking. Or, on a less extreme note, your would-be mate doesn't have those addictions, but does think about sex all the time, doesn't see a problem with passionate love scenes in PG-13 and R-rated movies, spends a lot of alone time with members of the opposite sex (they swear they don't touch, but are so close emotionally, it leaves you wondering), has no filter for inappropriate music, and, even though he or she hasn't technically had full-on sex with someone, thinks it's "fine" to mess around.

So, is this person still your dream husband or wife? If your answer is no, then consider this: **you attract what you are.**

If you could meet your future husband or wife—this afternoon—and you were able to ask them anything, what would you ask them about the choices they've made in the area of sexual purity?

Write your questions here (we've suggested one for you):

1. Have you saved sex for me?

2.

3.

4.

5.

6.

7.

8.

9.

10.

Now reread the questions you wrote. Write down your answers to those same questions—as if they were asked of you by your future husband or wife:

1.

2.

3.

4.

5.

6.

7.

8.

9.

10.

So ask yourself again: What kind of person do you want to have authority over your body? What kind of body do you want to give that person?

A story from our team:

From Isaac: Kelsey and I have quite a love story now, but you wouldn't have thought it possible from the ways our lives started out. Growing up in opposite ends of the world (I grew up in Southeast Asia, Kelsey grew up in the U.S.), life found us bouncing from one bad choice about sex, parties, and relationships to the next. Over time, we both came to know the Lord, and he began the long, painful road of restoration long before we ever met each other.

As I was following him, the Lord assured me that if I gave up the things of this world, he would in turn fulfill my every hope, longing, and desire. But before he could do that, I had to give it all to him: my time, my desires, my constant pursuit of relationships—all of it. Only when he had it all could he, in his perfect timing, give me what I needed.

God had placed a strong burden on me for my future wife, long before I ever met her. I started seeking him about how I could honor her, even though I had no idea who she was or when she was coming along. He prompted me to begin saving for my future wife's engagement ring. Now, this was a tall order. At the time I was a teen, barely making any money, but I did my best to be obedient. Month by month, I would set aside as much as I could into a savings account, even if it was only one dollar! As I did so, I'd pray for my future wife. Year by year, I saved and prayed that one day God would bring me someone I could spend my life with.

As I got to know Kelsey, I knew that she was the one I had been waiting for. Once I was confident that God had called us together as husband and wife, I went to the jeweler and picked out a beautiful ring. When I proposed and put that ring on her finger, I knew that God had answered every prayer I had prayed to bring me an awesome wife.

From Kelsey: When Isaac proposed, I couldn't believe it. It was so difficult for me to accept that God would bring me such an incredible husband after all the mistakes I had made.

My teen years began with a backpack full of good intentions and a desire to keep healthy boundaries; but little by little, my standards began to conform to those of the world. Before I knew it, lines were crossed, and feeling completely helpless, I found myself in the deepest, most despairing pit I had ever known. My heart, once filled with hopes and dreams, lay in a pile of broken pieces, surrounded with the insurmountable guilt of sex, lies, alcohol, attempted abortion—you name it, it was there.

When I was nineteen, the Lord got a hold of my life in a radical way. He placed such a desire in my heart to know him and seek him. As the rebuilding of my life began, I realized that I had done so much damage to my own heart and mind (not to mention body) that many basic "purity principles" had to be relearned. The Lord encouraged me to set up a high standard for my relationships, and one of those standards was for my first kiss in my next relationship to be on my wedding day. Remember, when God says he "makes all things new," that includes our purity! By his incredible love and forgiveness, he can restore that which has been lost.

I didn't know how I was going to reach this goal, but one thing I did know—I had to run after God and never look back. For me, that meant giving up everything I used to cling to, everything that had caused me to get tangled up. I lost every friend I had, I changed my phone number, my e-mail address, my clothing choices, the music I listened to, the movies I watched, and I even moved to a different state for a time. I did everything I could to make sure that I would never run back to the person I used to be. Over time, I made new friends, got involved in this incredible ministry, and rebuilt my life on Christ's foundation.

Seven years after the Lord saved my life, I stood at the entrance of the chapel doors, wearing a stunning white gown, smiling at my father. He squeezed my hand, we took a deep breath, and the massive glass doors opened to a petal-filled aisle that would lead me to Isaac. On that evening, in front of our closest friends and family, Isaac and I shared our very first kiss! And let me tell you—it was WELL worth the wait!

Never sell yourself short of the incredible love story God has for you. I truly believe that if you turn to him, he will run to you. We serve an incredible God who is mighty to save you from anything and everything that holds you back from him.

GUARD THE GATE

We once overheard a friend talking about how incredible her husband was going to be—but it never once crossed her mind that to attract an awesome guy, she'd have to be awesome too. If you are not the person you would want to share the rest of your life with, then things will need to change. This is not something you might, maybe, do *some*day. These things need to change right away. Why? The longer you wait, the harder it will be to change. Trust us on this one. Do yourself a favor and start now!

Imagine there's a transcript, a written record, of every thought that passes through your mind. Now imagine it gets projected onto a big screen at church on Sunday morning—just like the worship lyrics. OUCH. Does that scare you? We've been there—we know that fear.

But if your answer was yes, there is good news: there are some things you can do! **Romans 12:2 says: "Do not conform to the pattern of this world, but be transformed by the renewing of your mind. Then you will be able to test and approve what God's will is—his good, pleasing and perfect will."**

Why are our thoughts so important in staying sexually pure? Because our actions are driven by our thoughts. So the most important place to start making changes is figuring out the things we think about. This is why the Bible talks about renewing our minds every day.

Here are some ways you can renew your mind:

1. *Start reading the Bible every day*. Ideally one chapter or more. Why? Read Philippians 4:8 and 2 Timothy 3:16, 17.
2. *Memorize specific Scriptures.* The next time you think a thought that you wouldn't want projected on a big screen, start quoting Scripture. Seriously, this works! Example: You

can't get the steamy movie scene from last night out of your head (that love scene you shouldn't have been watching anyway). Memorize Ephesians 2:4, 5. Then, read it again. Read the whole chapter!

3. *Get a change of scenery.* If you can't get something (or someone) out of your mind, get your thoughts focused elsewhere. Distract yourself; occupy your mind with things of eternal value. Don't let the thoughts continue; refuse to allow yourself to go there mentally. Recognize that what goes on in your mind eventually comes out!

4. *Acknowledge your weak points*, and know what feeds your lust. If you're struggling to keep your thoughts pure, do you:

★ **WATCH MOVIES WITH NUDITY/SEXUALITY?**

★ **LISTEN TO MUSIC WITH EXPLICIT LYRICS?**

★ **HAVE HEAVY MAKE-OUT SESSIONS WITH YOUR BOYFRIEND/GIRLFRIEND?**

★ **LOOK AT PORN, OR EVEN JUST STEAL OCCASIONAL GLANCES, TELLING YOURSELF IT "WON'T HURT ANYTHING"?**

★ **ENGAGE IN SOLO SEX? (SOLO SEX NEVER HELPED ANYONE IN THE QUEST TO BE PURE. EVER.)**

★ **AVOID BEING AROUND A COMMUNITY OF BELIEVERS?**

5. *Get help.* Get an accountability partner, someone who is older, wiser, and a strong Christian—someone you can be completely honest with, and who is the same gender as you.

In addition to guarding your thought life, what about what's going on with you physically? We know what it's like—sometimes it just seems like there is no room for Jesus in between you and your girlfriend or boyfriend. Here's some practical advice:

1. *Be honest.* With your accountability partner, be honest about the state of your relationship with your girlfriend or boyfriend. We're not going to lie—this is an absolute must if you want to stay physically pure.

2. *Establish physical limits.* Don't do anything physically that you would be ashamed of if your parents walked into the room. If you're still not sure how far is too far, how about you demonstrate in front of your pastors? . . . Wow—is it us, or did it just get hotter in here? Seriously though, we encourage you to aim for high standards of physical purity. One thing that's kept our team on the right track is that each of us has committed to not even kissing until the wedding day.

3. *Keep yourself out of compromising situations*—like being ALONE together! Don't watch movies with, drive with, or spend time—in any way!—with your date if no one else is around. Often couples find themselves compromising their standards simply because they happen to have the opportunity to do it.

4. *Have a plan*, and communicate with your accountability partner. If you have someone looking out for you, you're much less likely to find time to mess around.

5. *Know when to get out.* If the person you're with is pressuring you physically, it's time to get out of the relationship. Someone who truly cares about you won't pressure you into doing things sexually. Recognize that by pressuring you, that person is only looking out for number one—and that isn't you.

Another huge factor in staying sexually pure is the people around you. Do you ever feel pressured to please your surrounding audience? Your friends carry so much influence. Can you recognize the people in your life who are pulling you down? We all like to think we're the ones who will do the influencing, but sadly, that's not always the case.

Something else we've observed is that some of our friends may not want to see us successfully walking in purity—because they themselves aren't. If we get our act cleaned up, it might show how much improving *they* need. (See Ephesians 5:13.) So if your friends pull you down, realize why. Sometimes it's better to walk away from that friend or group of friends than to continue to let them pull you down to their standard.

What about your lifestyle? The people you hang with, the way you live your life—is that honoring to your future husband or wife? Would you do that if he or she were standing next to you? Live like your future spouse is watching.

You can also honor your future spouse now with your time. But you're probably saying: "I'm years away from that. What in the world do you mean?"

Instead of being down that you're the "only one" not dating, take time to pray for your relationships. Or take a cue from our friends Eric and Leslie Ludy and write love letters to your future spouse.

Can you imagine how incredible you would feel if, on your honeymoon, your husband or wife handed you a stack of letters and told you how they had been praying for you for years? That would be so cool! You could trust that they would be faithful to you for a lifetime, because they had already been so faithful all those years!

We encourage you to aim for the highest standard! As a team, we have committed to holding off on the whole dating thing, avoiding questionable situations, and last but not least, saving the first kiss for our weddings. We can tell you—it has been so worth it! God has met us powerfully because of our promise to walk pure with him.

1. Take a moment and reflect on your decisions in the past. Are you happy with the choices you've made in your romantic relationships? Reflect on why you feel this way.

2. What kind of relationship do you want to have in the future? Dream some here.

3. What in you needs to change to get this relationship? Are you the kind of person you'd want to marry? Be brutally honest.

MY JOURNAL

Look up Psalm 55:22. What are your cares? How often have you felt like you're in this battle for purity alone? What things will help you not feel alone?

Does the thought of staying pure in our world today overwhelm you? Be encouraged! God is on your side! Memorize Philippians 1:6. Who began the "good work" in you? Write, sketch, or dream about what good work you might accomplish. Think about people who are helping you to be who God made you to be—who do you want to be like?

CHALLENGE

What do you need to change? Self-evaluations are beautiful, insightful—and sometimes horribly painful! But without them, it's absolutely difficult to change or grow. Answer the questions below, and share them with your mentor. You may need to look back at these questions sometimes, even frequently. We are human—we tend to conveniently forget and fall back into our old way of doing things! Most importantly: pray about the issues you struggle with and ask Jesus to help you. You'll need his help!

1. *Thoughts*: When was the last time you thought about having sex? or had a lustful thought about someone? When was the last time you imagined yourself kissing someone, dating that amazing guy or girl, hugging your crush, or being asked out? How are you taking "captive every thought to make it obedient to Christ" (2 Corinthians 10:5)?

2. *Actions*: When was the last time you engaged in solo sex? or touched someone inappropriately? When was the last time you "checked someone out"? or said something suggestive? Have you been texting messages or posting things on the Internet that you know you shouldn't? Is there anything that has been done recently that you wouldn't want your parents to find out about?

3. *Entertainment choices*: When was the last time you looked at porn? When was the last time you watched a sexually explicit movie or scene? When was the last time you hung out somewhere where people were behaving in morally inappropriate ways? What kind of music lyrics are on your favorites list these days? Is the media you're consuming growing your relationship with God?

4. *Dating standards*: When you hang out with the opposite sex, are they friends or "more than friends"? Have you toyed with the thought of—or involved yourself in—twisted relationships that the world calls "friends with benefits"? Are you keeping your friendships as just friendships or are you always on the lookout for "the one"?

5. *Friends*: Are you compromising your standards by hanging out with the wrong people? When was the last time friends influenced a bad decision you made? How were they able to do it? Are you hanging out with people who are glorifying God?

After you've finished your evaluation, ask yourself this: Based on what we've talked about, what are ways you can change? What practical steps can you take? It could mean switching your movie or music choices. It could mean not reading your sports magazine because the models cause you to stumble. Take a good, serious look at your entertainment choices. Are they filled with sex or behavior you wouldn't want to copy?

All of us on our team have been in the same situation you've been in: stuck in a theater with friends who don't seem to care about the sexual content/nudity and crude jokes. So what did we do? We left. Did it make us stand out? Yes. Did we sometimes have to call someone to get a ride? You bet. Was it worth it? Absolutely. Because that night during devotions, we could honestly say, "Lord, I tried my hardest to keep my mind pure." Instead of being plagued with sexual thoughts, we were able to focus on other things, because we chose not to fill our minds with garbage.

Purity pledge

Have you committed to purity before? Even if you have and failed miserably, it's never too late to start over. That's the beauty of God's grace. We wrote this pledge to be like a prayer. We encourage you to pray this, sign it, and also have your accountability partner sign it.

If you'd like to write your own, one that's worded the way you wish, we encourage you to do so! Or add additional thoughts to this one. Need a reminder? Consider wearing a ring symbolizing purity as a daily reminder of your commitment.

Dear God, I know I've made mistakes in the area of purity. Help me realize how much you care about me and how much you care about who I marry. Give me the strength to wait for who you have for me. Give me the grace I need to stand strong against temptation. Help me as I work to deny the areas of impurity that I've fed and held onto. Give me a hatred for the sexual impurity that's around me. Lord, help me love the things you love and hate the things that you hate. With your help, I commit to being faithful to Jesus, and to walk in the calling and destiny that he has in store for me. Amen.

_____

Your Signature   Date

_____

Accountability Partner   Date

Take a moment to think of five specific ways you want to stay pure. Here are some of our examples:

1. I'm dedicating my body to the Lord and to my future spouse, and I commit to guarding my body for the purposes God has for me.

2. My eyes belong to the Lord, and I commit to guarding them against things that would cause me to stumble, or that have even a hint of impurity.

3. I commit to saving my first kiss for my wedding day.

4. I choose to discipline my mind and keep it pure for the plans and purpose of God.

5. I commit to staying accountable to the people that God has around me.

Now you give it a shot. Write five ways you want to stay pure:

1.

2.

3.

4.

5.

A story from our team:

I (Kelsey) was on a Caribbean cruise with my closest friends and family when I had a unique opportunity to share about my commitment to purity. Staff for the boat had been nearby all during our last evening at sea, and as we were about to leave, I struck up a conversation with the ship's emcee. (An emcee on a cruise ship is typically a young, very charismatic character who announces the ship's activities and hosts parties on board.)

"What do you do?" he asked.

"I work for a ministry in the U.S.," I replied, forgetting what the word *ministry* often means to foreigners.

"Oh, so like the Ministry of Education or Health?" he questioned.

"Well, we do educate . . . but it is actually a Christian ministry. To help young people be pure." The look of surprise on his face was so unusual. He had honestly never heard of this concept.

"Are you married?" When I said no, he asked, "Then why are you wearing a ring on your finger?" He pointed to my purity ring.

And so the conversation began. We went on to discuss how, in this day and age, this lifestyle of purity could even be possible, because to this young man, it wasn't possible. After several moments of discussion, he sighed heavily and confessed, "It is just too difficult. I can't do that."

What struck me about his response was the familiarity of it. This young man was lost. Without a Savior. His answer was far from rare. In fact, I hear it often among

Christian teens and young adults. How is it that we, as the body of Christ, are giving the same defeated answer as our lost friends?

Allow me to offer a disclaimer: I'm not an expert on purity; I have had my share of defeats and victories in this arena. So the following information is not intended to claim my perfection, only my determination.

The difficulty in remaining pure in our culture today rests heavily, if not solely, on our indecision. Now before you line up your arguments for or against that statement, keep reading. The moment you are determined to face something, with the power of the Lord Jesus, no force on earth can stop you. Victory is yours for the taking.

The enemy is so keenly aware of this truth that his number-one tactic is to convince you that Christ's standards are unattainable.

Culture never ceases to remind us that it is impractical, impossible, and illogical to remain pure. But what culture does not want to tell you is that believing these lies places you neck-deep in enemy territory, rendering you nearly useless. What happened to the freedom gained for Christians by Jesus' self-sacrifice at Calvary? Just because we live in the here and now instead of ancient Bible times doesn't give us the excuse: "It's different now. Those rules of what's right and wrong don't apply." They absolutely do apply, now more than ever.

So how does this work? How do we remain pure? Let me give you a glimpse of a personal victory in my life. For years I had struggled with going back to the same sins and I could never understand why. The drive for holiness was there, but the wisdom needed to achieve it was not.

At that time, God began speaking to me through his Word and very wise mentors about tracing my thoughts. The idea of tracing goes like this. Whenever you experience troublesome or sinful thoughts, you stop, go back in your steps and in your mind, and try to identify when these thoughts began: *When did this happen? Who was I with? What was I doing?* Let's use this example: I could be having a great week regarding victories in purity of heart, mind, and body. Friday night rolls around and I go out with friends. By the end of the night, I'm left feeling like I am incomplete without a significant other. *STOP*, I tell myself. *THINK.*

If I'm with people who are unguarded and all of them are looking for a quick fling, it's no wonder I'm left with this empty desire. Here's a crazy idea, I tell myself: *Stop hanging out with those people.* I will tell you this: the best thing I ever did was walk away from the people who were causing me to stumble, because nothing on earth is worth losing ground with Christ.

Thoughts from the team:

Ponder this scenario: If you were truly to decide to stand firm in Christ, and if the Bible is right, and if God is not a liar, then that means that you are **"more than conquerors through him who loved us" (Romans 8:37).** And that includes conquering ourselves for the sake of our purity. Next time you begin thinking that it's too difficult to remain pure in our world, begin tracing your thoughts—and remember the truth of this verse.

These are the things that impacted me the most from this session:

These are the things I'm still struggling with, that I need to wrestle with in prayer:

"WHO SHALL SEPARATE US FROM THE LOVE OF CHRIST? SHALL TROUBLE OR HARDSHIP OR PERSECUTION OR FAMINE OR NAKEDNESS OR DANGER OR SWORD?" —ROMANS 8:35

PART FIVE

ESCAPING NORMAL

During your Culture Shock experience, we pray that God plants a seed deep within your heart that will encourage you to passionately pursue your calling in him. Allow this last study to challenge you and shape you like never before. Don't miss this incredible opportunity to be refined and sharpened.

Remember that if we're going to be in this world but not of it, we're going to have to realize that what most of us have been accepting as normal is NOT what God ever had in mind for us. The world's view of *normal* is so far from how awesome life *could be* that we should never compromise—we have to escape it. So what are you waiting for? Nothing is holding you back from the crazy adventure that God has in store for you.

Step one? Escape normal.

RENEWING YOUR MIND

What are you passionate about? What do you want to get involved in? We all desire to do great things. We all want to be recognized and have good reputations. But the real question is: Are we willing to serve?

Let's take this example: A couple of teens are really passionate about a certain politician, so they decide to help with the campaign. But problems surface when they walk through the doors with the idea that they are going to *run* the show. By day five, they're getting coffee for the phone operators and are asked to stuff envelopes for hours on end—and by day six, they are super offended! *This is so stupid*, they think. *We should be doing the REAL jobs, not this mindless junk!*

The problem is this: Somewhere in our culture we've gotten this idea that we don't have to start at the bottom. We think, *Sure, the whole servanthood thing is great for some people, but I'm the exception. I have skills. I have talents. And the people I am working for better notice me or else! The normal rules don't apply to me. I am different.*

Maybe it's our society that has given us this sense of entitlement—that we have the right to certain privileges. Or maybe it's not our society. Maybe it's just our pride. Think about it: Are your motives to further the kingdom of God, or are

> **"LISTEN TO ADVICE AND ACCEPT DISCIPLINE, AND AT THE END YOU WILL BE COUNTED AMONG THE WISE." — PROVERBS 19:20**

they to look really good to everyone and be the "super-amazing, so-incredibly-awesome hero" of everything?

If the Bible clearly tells us the key to being great is to be a servant, why are we not all practicing this? If Jesus so clearly spoke to his disciples about servanthood, why don't we all jump on board? (Check out Matthew 20:20-28 for a great story on this involving Jesus and his disciples.)

Could it be that the idea of being a servant just seems beneath us? Could it be we value ourselves so highly that we're too good to do a little hard work? Or maybe we just are afraid of the person we might have to serve—after all, it could be anyone: a boss, a teacher, a homeless person, that kid in fifth period who drives us up the wall . . .

What does being a servant mean to you? One thing is for sure: it's *not* simply performing a single, random good deed. It's not this: "One time, I stayed after youth group to help clean up. Now I can check the 'being a servant' thing off my list. Done and done." Being a servant isn't something that you can cross off your life's to-do list—ever.

Choose to serve those around you day in and day out. They may be your parents, your boss, your family, your pastor, or your siblings. Even great leaders must remember that they are always in the position to serve.

The enemy hates that fact about Christians. He will always set out to make you feel mistreated. He will always whisper in your ear, "This is *so* not fair! You don't deserve this! Why are you the only one who has to do this?" In those moments, remember one very key thing: not everyone (or even anyone) you serve will be perfect. At some point you are going to feel mistreated or walked all over, but the learning and growth that come from humbling yourself and submitting during those hard times is worth its weight in gold.

Don't forget how badly people treated Jesus. Take heart; he has been there. And he is encouraging you to follow him.

REFLECT/DISCUSS

1. Are you willing to serve when no one else is watching? What if you never get credit for it? How would you feel about serving then?

2. Can you think of anything you can do (*without* getting credit for it), whether it's for your parents, your church, your teachers, or others, that would really bless them this week? Seek out those opportunities this week, and watch God move in your life! Write about that thing here and challenge yourself to make it happen.

Whoever wants to be first

Our pastor once told our team: "God can get a lot more done when it doesn't matter who gets the credit." That struck us all really hard. Would we be willing to do all the hard work and then let someone else get all the glory? Our goal is to be able to answer that question with a resounding yes!

Jesus really wasn't kidding when he told his disciples that they had to be servants if they wanted to become great. He didn't say, "If you want to be great, then it might be a good idea if you learned to serve." It's nonnegotiable. Matthew 20:26-28: **"Whoever wants to become great among you must be your servant, and whoever wants to be first must be your slave—just as the Son of Man did not come to be served, but to serve, and to give his life as a ransom for many."**

Our example is Christ. If the creator of the universe humbled himself and took the servant's position, what makes us think we don't have to? Not a single being on this earth is better or higher than God. If he had to do it, then we do also.

If you look at strong men and women of the New Testament and from the church history that followed, you see that they often started at the very bottom. Jesus said, "Whoever wants to be first must be your slave," and great servants throughout history took that verse and ran with it. They weren't in it for the glory, fame, or recognition. They served because they had a passion for Jesus Christ and nothing else mattered, not even their reputations. Greatness only comes after we have become servants, and we are only able to be true servants after we have given up the desire to be recognized and honored for the work that we do. God is looking for someone who will give the glory right back to him. Are you willing to do that?

Ask God to give you an opportunity to serve. We're talking about doing the things no one else wants to do (and quite possibly not getting paid for it!). If you get discouraged, think of this: The famous missionary Gladys Aylward spent two years cleaning houses *after* she knew God had called her to China. Sometimes God gives us a passion for something and then he asks us to do something really strange: give it back to him.

"What?!" you might ask. "Why would God want me to give up the desire that *he* placed in my heart?" Because God has the big picture in mind—he has a far greater plan for your life than you could ever imagine. He alone knows the kind of training you need. He knows when you are ready to take on the massive responsibility of your calling, and he knows what you have to go through to get ready for it.

Which brings us to another very important—but again, unpopular—point: God's education system is different from ours. God is not limited to a classroom. What we think of as an education is not always the way God sees it. You may have aced every class, but if your character isn't developed, do you think you will be useful in his kingdom? That isn't to say that we shouldn't be pouring effort into our academic education, because we absolutely need to! But we also have to pour as much energy into growing our relationship with the Lord and growing in virtue as we do learning in the academic classroom.

An older version of *Webster's Dictionary* gives this classic definition of virtue[6]: **"Virtue is nothing but voluntary obedience to truth."** But we will never learn to be obedient without a strong foundation of character. That is why we have to pursue building our character with all of our hearts. If we don't invest time in our character and the learning of obedience, we won't stick to it when the going gets tough!

Max Lucado said: "God doesn't call the qualified, He qualifies the called" (*Outlive Your Life*)[7]. And it's true. If God tells you to do something, he will provide the training you need to do it. He's faithful that way.

Have you ever thought about the fact that God knows how to do everything? Absolutely *everything*. He created the brains that launched the first ship into outer space. He created the hands that painted the ceiling of the Sistine Chapel. He also did something no one else has ever done: he created an entire world. So the next time God tells you to do something and you don't know how to do it, why not ask him for direction? And when you rely on him, totally, completely, for strength and wisdom to accomplish the task before you, you'll see him work wonders in your life. But don't stop there. Give God the credit.

Be available for whatever God brings along. Be ready to serve in any area, whether it is noticeable or hidden. You may be serving in the lowest of the low positions, or God may call you to a position of great responsibility. Be ready to be a servant.

One time our team was hosting a group of Christian leaders—and impressive ones, at that—at our pastor's home. After dinner, one of the more famous gentlemen walked over to the sink and started doing the dishes from the meal! We were shocked! But that was a truly incredible moment for us. This man was well known by everyone, yet he didn't think himself too high to simply serve. It was a great example of Christ's attitude, and we are aiming to follow it every day!

REFLECT/DISCUSS

1. What are you passionate about? What are some things you would like to do in your lifetime?

2. Can you think of anyone in history who did amazing things for God *and* had the approval of his peers the whole time? Think of a time when you didn't have the approval of your peers, yet you knew you were doing the right thing. Was it worth it? What made it worth doing? Or if it wasn't worth it, why not? Would you do it again?

3. What is your reputation worth to you? Think of a situation in which you let your reputation get in the way of doing what you knew God would have wanted you to do. If you were placed in that same situation today, what would you do differently?

Honestly evaluate your reaction to people's disapproval of you. Although it can be hurtful or even frustrating, how do you react to someone's disapproval of you? Check out Matthew 10:22. What feelings or thoughts does this verse bring to your heart and mind?

Make your own definition of a servant, and write it below. These verses can help shape your definition: Luke 16:13; John 13:3-5; 15:20; Romans 14:4; 15:8; Galatians 1:10; Colossians 3:22.

Say you have a strong desire to minister in Africa, but God has not yet opened that door for you. What can you do if you are unable to go right now? Look up Matthew 10:38. Write down some things that you can do to prepare yourself now. How can you take up your cross and be ready to follow Jesus?

THE LITTLE THINGS

The following is an activity that will help you identify your God-given gifts. The apostle Paul outlined some of the great gifts that God gives. He wrote:

> For just as each of us has one body with many members, and these members do not all have the same function, so in Christ we, though many, form one body, and each member belongs to all the others. We have different gifts, according to the grace given to each of us. If your gift is prophesying, then prophesy in accordance with your faith; if it is serving, then serve; if it is teaching, then teach; if it is to encourage, then give encouragement; if it is giving, then give generously; if it is to lead, do it diligently; if it is to show mercy, do it cheerfully. (Romans 12:4-8)

Let's set the stage with some fun. The numbered statements below correspond to the numbered gifts shown below those. Pretend for a moment that you and your friends are playing a little football in your mom's kitchen. Just as a friend goes long for a pass, he trips and knocks the fruit bowl all over the counter, sending an orange flying across the room, knocking over his soda in the process. Which one of these most closely matches how you would react? Choose one:

1. "I knew that was going to happen!"
2. "Oh no! Let me go get you a new drink and some paper towels."
3. "Do you know why you spilled that? I think I can help you figure it out."
4. "Don't worry—this kind of thing happens to everyone. You'll be more careful next time, I'm sure."
5. "Here, you can have mine since yours spilled."
6. "Greg—napkins. Kim—water. Charlie—get another soda for him, please."

7. "Aw, I hate when that happens to me. Did it spill on you? I'm sure it will all be OK; my mom won't mind."

Match the number of your reaction with the numbered explanation to help you identify your gifts.

1. *Prophecy*: You tune in to what God has to say. Study the Scriptures and the history of God's people so that you can better know how to prepare for what's happening in the church. Don't be afraid to speak out when you see God working in others. Join or, better yet, *create* a support team for teens who are out to do great things for God! Team up with an adult leader and help people around you fulfill their calling.

The Little Things: Do you see people around you making bad choices? Pray for them, and find a Scripture that will help them understand the path they are on. Ask God to help you have the right words to say. You never know, a simple prayer or a few words of wisdom might change their lives.

2. *Serving*: There are places to serve all over the place! The nursing home, soup kitchen, church, and many more. Remember, even Jesus did not come to be served but to serve! No one can truly be like Christ unless he or she is willing to serve first. Truly having a servant's outlook on life can start in your very own home. Write out ten different ways you can serve your parents each day this week.

The Little Things: Sometimes we get trapped in the mentality that we should only do something if there's a reward involved. But God specifically says he will reward what is done in secret. (Check out Matthew 6:1-4!) Don't just join the big service team at church; look for small opportunities to serve everywhere. Try picking up the trash in the parking lot. No one will notice you did it, but God absolutely will, and he will reward you accordingly!

3. *Teaching*: Help out in your Sunday school ministry. Kids are hungry to learn about everything! Even if you're a teacher's aide, you can change the life of so many children. Here's a cool idea: We've noticed that many kids aren't up on their Bible facts. Do some research and present some facts to your church's children's director and maybe you can teach the kids these fun facts as well.

The Little Things: The best way to become a good teacher is to learn as much as you can. Don't assume you're the expert. Read as many books as you can and, more than anything, study and memorize the Bible. There will be times when you don't know how to teach someone, but God knows exactly what everyone needs. Having those memory verses ready can help you help others later.

4. *Encouragement*: Pray about starting a Bible study with peers, friends, or those younger than you. Go to www.generationsofvirtue.org to find awesome Bible studies that will encourage you and those around you to live a life of purity.

The Little Things: As people are learning and growing in their own faith, sometimes the best thing you can do is just pray for them. Make sure your positivity doesn't gloss over real needs or areas where people need to change. Let God be the encourager to all—one who gives strong advice, warnings, or firm urgings—and you focus on being a prayer warrior and helper!

5. *Giving*: What a wonderful way to show God's love! Give to those who cannot get for themselves. You don't have to spend a lot of money to give generously. With a few ingredients and some friends, you can whip up several dozen cookies in no time. Fill paper plates or plastic bags with some cookies and take them to a homeless shelter in your area. Another idea: you probably have a hundred things in your room and closet that you never use. Bag up those things and distribute them to a homeless shelter or charity thrift store near you. Bless someone who can't afford to buy that shirt or new notebook.

The Little Things: What you give doesn't always have a price tag. A smile or kind word can go a long way. Spend some time and make a list of the little things you can give to brighten someone's day. If you make a pattern of this, it will become second nature, and you'll be able to impact people no matter what you're doing. Remember that sometimes, what people need most is for you to give of yourself.

6. *Leading*: Use your leadership talent to coach a team or put on a play. Get your friends together and find a lesser-known Bible story and make a performance out of it. Or hold a basketball tournament and give the proceeds to a local charity. Maybe you could coach a sports skills camp or volunteer as a leader for a summer camp. Trust us, when you speak, people will listen. Use your voice and gifting to lead and encourage the

people around you right now. Don't just think about your friends and peers; remember the younger kids too.

The Little Things: Every good leader has been, at one time, a careful follower. And just because you *can* lead doesn't mean you always should. Step back from some of your self-appointed responsibilities and be still. Get quiet enough before God that you can hear his whisper. Allow others around you to lead, and practice supporting them in that, no matter what.

7. *Showing Mercy*: Join or start a prayer group. Use your gift of mercy to show compassion to those who are in distress and pray for them. Because of your mercy gift, many people will feel like they can freely pour their hearts out to you. Pray for those who are confiding in you. But remember, although confidentiality is important, if a person tells you something that could be harmful, be sure to tell a trusted adult leader.

The Little Things: While your strength might be showing mercy, don't allow yourself to be taken advantage of by those seeking to trample you. And as people confide in you, don't carry their troubles all on your shoulders alone. Through prayer, talk to Jesus about these burdens and allow him to work in your heart and in the lives of those around you.

Since God gave you the incredible gifts he did, you can be sure he has a definite plan for using them for his glory and to build up his kingdom. He has an awesome plan and purpose for your life, so go for it!

Look once more at the gifts outlined in this activity. Do you feel one of them is really yours? Or maybe more than one? Is there one that just screams your name? Do you believe you have a gift that is similar in nature to one of these, if not exactly the same? Unsure? Ask your parents, mentors, youth leaders, or a friend!

There's no question God has given you gifts. Seek them out! Take a minute to journal how you feel God could use your gifts and abilities:

Samuel said to Saul, "I am the one the LORD sent to anoint you king over his people Israel; so listen now to the message from the LORD. This is what the LORD Almighty says: 'I will punish the Amalekites for what they did to Israel when they waylaid them as they came up from Egypt. Now go, attack the Amalekites and totally destroy all that belongs to them. Do not spare them; put to death men and women, children and infants, cattle and sheep, camels and donkeys.'"

So Saul summoned the men and mustered them at Telaim—two hundred thousand foot soldiers and ten thousand from Judah. Saul went to the city of Amalek and set an ambush in the ravine. Then he said to the Kenites, "Go away, leave the Amalekites so that I do not destroy you along with them; for you showed kindness to all the Israelites when they came up out of Egypt." So the Kenites moved away from the Amalekites.

Then Saul attacked the Amalekites all the way from Havilah to Shur, near the eastern border of Egypt. He took Agag king of the Amalekites alive, and all his people he totally destroyed with the sword. But Saul and the army spared Agag and the best of the sheep and cattle, the fat calves and lambs—everything that was good. These they were unwilling to destroy completely, but everything that was despised and weak they totally destroyed. (1 Samuel 15:1-9)

King Saul was leading the Israelites in a war against the Amalekites, who were enemies of the people of God, the Jews. The prophet Samuel told King Saul not to let any of the Amalekites live, because the intentions of their hearts were completely evil toward God and his people. This seems harsh, but as we'll find out, God knew what he was doing. He also told King Saul not to take any of the Amalekites' belongings, but to destroy all of them, because they were so defiled.

A good guess would be that the Amalekites' stuff captured after the battle must've seemed almost good to resist. But if it were actually irresistible, God never would have required this of them (check out 1 Corinthians 10:13). Before we judge the actions the Israelites chose, a question for anyone to answer is: how do you think you'd behave in their shoes? You've just gone through a horrendous, violent battle. You go to chuck all your enemy's junk into a huge burn barrel, until you have the realization: *This stuff is worth something!* You can't just burn this stuff . . . come on! Maybe it's a little like the time you went garage-sale shopping with your mom and found that prized piece of someone else's junk! You've just got to do something with it! Except, in the case of the Israelites, God told them to have *nothing* to do with it. But they made possessions their idol . . . sound familiar?

The Israelites just wouldn't listen. They couldn't bear to see such treasure simply destroyed. No matter that God had warned them to obey and to get rid of it all. They ignored the fact that their history proved that disobedience would be a disaster for them. In the heat of the moment, they didn't think of any of that. So they begged their beloved king to let them go through with their well-thought-out (or so they thought) plan. And he agreed.

Tragically, Saul took the disobedience a step further. Not only did he concede to the will of the people, he went so far as to allow the Amalekite king, Agag, to live. When the prophet Samuel caught wind of King Saul's actions, he was furious. Samuel then person-ally took care of Agag the way Saul should have, and it wasn't long before Saul lost his entire kingdom to a man who, while not perfect, was willing to obey God at all costs. And even when he fell short, he sincerely repented. This man was the shepherd boy who would one day be king, David.

The terrifying outcome of this story comes when we understand that the actions of King Saul affected more than just those in his lifetime. Let's fast-forward nearly 500 years later to when the events of the book of Esther took place.

Esther, a Jew in hiding, miraculously becomes queen in a less-than-customary manner. (It's quite a story; check out Esther, chapters 1 and 2.) She later hears word from her uncle Mordecai that her husband's right-hand advisor, Haman, has a plan that will wipe out her entire race. This is no small thing, not just a group of people in some danger. No, it's the *entire Jewish race*.

Esther, while anxiously fasting and praying, goes to the king to confess the truth about her heritage and to beg for mercy on behalf of her people. She went to the king unsummoned, which in those days could carry the penalty of death.

Esther's courage and bravery saved her people and made her a woman that the world will never forget, especially the Jews, who observe the celebration of Purim every year in her honor.

Her actions led to Haman's being executed in the same way in which he had planned to kill Mordecai. But what if Esther—like Saul—had copped out of her calling? What if she had bowed down to man's approval? What if she too had chosen to do what she wanted?

You see, Esther was a direct descendant of King Saul. Scholars believe that Haman was an Agagite, and a direct descendant of the royal line of King Agag. So it took hundreds of years, from King Agag to Esther, to complete the job that Saul left unfinished.

Don't ever believe that your calling is any less significant than King David's or Queen Esther's, no matter what the future looks like to you. Let's not slack off on the calling God has placed on our lives. Who knows how many lives can be changed for good or for bad, depending on what we choose?

Esther 1:19 says, "Let the king give her royal position to someone else who is better than she." This is what the king said when he was looking for a new queen to replace his former, disobedient wife. The woman he eventually found was Esther. What does that verse say to you?

Consider for a moment the reality of your calling. If you don't fulfill it, it will be given to someone else. You have an amazing opportunity. The only question now is, will you take it?

GREAT RESOURCES

★ YOU CAN READ MORE ABOUT ESTHER'S BEAUTIFUL AND AMAZING STORY IN THE BOOK OF ESTHER. WE HIGHLY SUGGEST YOU CHECK IT OUT!

★ IF YOU CAN, WATCH A PORTION OF THE MOVIE *ONE NIGHT WITH THE KING* FOR A VISUAL ILLUSTRATION OF THE STORY OF ESTHER.

REFLECT/DISCUSS

1. Have you noticed that sometimes it seems as if others get away with total, blatant disobedience, just like King Saul did? Can you give examples? (If you're in a discussion group, do not use any specific names.)

2. Look up Psalm 73. What does this chapter tell you about how our perception of sin changes when it looks like people around us can do whatever they want and get away with it?

3. Read Psalm 14:5 (*AMP*): "There they shall be in great fear [literally—dreading a dread], for God is with the generation of the [uncompromisingly] righteous (those upright and in right standing with Him)." What do you think it means to be uncompromisingly righteous? What do you think a generation can accomplish if God is present with them?

MY JOURNAL

Have you ever thought you were nothing special, with no reason for being on earth? Do you feel this way now? Think about, journal about, pray about, talk about, or draw about that time. What did or does it feel like? Why do you think you felt, or feel, that way?

From the Scriptures shared throughout this Culture Shock event, what is God's view of you? What can you do to see yourself more through God's eyes?

DESTINY STEALERS

The enemy will always come at you by trying to tempt you with the areas where you're weakest. We call these areas "destiny stealers." Maybe your destiny stealer is sex. Or money. Or popularity. Whatever it is, the enemy doesn't play fair, and he *will* use your shortcomings against you. That's why it's so critical to allow God to come in and expose those areas filled with darkness so that they can overflow with light.

Often, the things we struggle with the most are the things God wants to give us the biggest victories in. Do not believe—for one second—that these victories are not worth fighting for. Whatever you struggle with, however difficult the battle, it is *so* worth fighting against the darkness so that you can walk in Christ's light.

But before we can escape normal, we have to recognize and understand what our destiny stealers are to begin with. We have to take a healthy evaluation of ourselves before we can repent and move away from the old mind-sets and habits. It is absolutely worth taking the time to inwardly examine your heart, because remember, although destiny stealers may not seem to be any big deal, Satan actually uses them to destroy your future. Here are the more common destiny stealers we have encountered:

* *LUST AND SEXUAL IMMORALITY*: THESE WERE AT THE ROOT OF KING SOLOMON'S DOWNFALL. PICTURE A PERFECTLY ENTERTAINING MOVIE WITH A ROTTEN ENDING. SUCH WAS THE TRAGIC END OF SOLOMON'S LIFE. IN SPITE OF GOD'S WARNING, THE BIBLE TELLS US THAT KING SOLOMON LOVED MANY FOREIGN WOMEN (1 KINGS 11:1, 2). IN FACT, WE'RE TOLD THAT HE HAD 700 WIVES AND 300 CONCUBINES (BASICALLY, MISTRESSES), AND THESE WOMEN LED HIM ASTRAY. AS HE GREW OLDER, HIS WIVES TURNED HIS HEART AFTER OTHER GODS, AND HIS HEART WAS NO LONGER FULLY DEVOTED TO HIS GOD (1 KINGS 11:3, 4).

* *PRIDE*: C. S. LEWIS DEFINED PRIDE AS "THE COMPLETE ANTI-GOD STATE OF MIND" (*MERE CHRISTIANITY*)[8]. THROUGH PRIDE, A PERSON WILL ATTEMPT TO EXALT HIMSELF OR HERSELF ABOVE GOD AND, IN DOING SO, SAY "I DON'T NEED GOD." HERE ARE SOME VERSES THAT WARN US AGAINST PRIDE: "PRIDE GOES BEFORE DESTRUCTION, AND HAUGHTINESS BEFORE A FALL" (PROVERBS 16:18) AND "BUT HE GIVES US EVEN MORE GRACE TO STAND AGAINST SUCH EVIL DESIRES. AS THE SCRIPTURES SAY, 'GOD OPPOSES THE PROUD BUT FAVORS THE HUMBLE'" (JAMES 4:6, *NLT*).

* *GREED*: SECOND KINGS 5 TELLS US THE STORY OF THE PROPHET ELISHA'S SERVANT GEHAZI. GEHAZI WAS NEXT IN LINE TO RECEIVE ELISHA'S MANTLE, JUST AS ELISHA RECEIVED HIS MANTLE FROM ELIJAH. HE WAS ON COURSE TO FULFILLING HIS CALLING AND DESTINY—IF IT WERE NOT FOR GREED. HE ACCEPTED MONEY AND CLOTHING FROM THE GENTILE GENERAL, NAAMAN, WHEN HIS MASTER ELISHA SPECIFICALLY INSTRUCTED HIM NOT TO DO SO. IN DOING THIS, GEHAZI FORFEITED HIS CALLING AND TRAGICALLY LIVED OUT THE REST OF HIS LIFE AS A LEPER. WHAT COULD'VE BECOME OF GEHAZI HAD HE NOT ENTERTAINED GREED AND THE DESIRE FOR MATERIAL POSSESSIONS? HE LOST HIS SPOT IN THE HALL OF FAME OF PROPHETS BECAUSE OF HIS GREED.

What do you feel are your biggest destiny stealers? They might be those just listed, similar to them, or different ones. Journal here:

How can you overcome the destiny stealers in your life?

Now is the time to take these destiny stealers to the foot of the cross and ask for Christ's help. We need to put on the armor of God (Ephesians 6) and stand against the things that want to destroy us. Quick, read that last part again. *The destiny stealers in your life are out to destroy you*. This isn't some small, little thing that doesn't really matter; these are *huge* battles. But there isn't reason to fear or worry. Christ wants to walk alongside you, if you'll open yourself to him and ask for his help.

The choices and decisions you're making right now will have eternal implications. If you choose to stand against the things in your life that seek to destroy you, you'll be able to save yourself from the heartache and pain that destiny stealers cause. By choosing to walk in purity, in honesty, and in holiness at this age, you are literally blessing your future.

From now on, guard yourself against the lies of the enemy that say that the destiny stealers in your life won't hurt you or that standing for righteousness is just being too extreme. We assure you: whatever is inside you that is a refuge for the lies of the enemy must be rooted out. And the amazing part of all of this is that God absolutely can do it! He—more than anyone on earth—knows your potential and longs for you to fulfill your destiny.

He is the author of your life's story, with all the intense moments and beautiful turns that make your life uniquely yours. So trust him. Trust him that he has your absolute best in mind. Trust that, day by day and decision by decision, he will help you escape normal—forever.

MY JOURNAL

These are the things that impacted me the most from this session:

These are the things I'm still struggling with, that I need to wrestle with in prayer:

> **"CONSIDER IT PURE JOY, MY BROTHERS AND SISTERS, WHENEVER YOU FACE TRIALS OF MANY KINDS, BECAUSE YOU KNOW THAT THE TESTING OF YOUR FAITH PRODUCES PERSEVERANCE. LET PERSEVERANCE FINISH ITS WORK SO THAT YOU MAY BE MATURE AND COMPLETE, NOT LACKING ANYTHING." —JAMES 1:2-4**

CULTURE SHOCK REWIND

We hope you've had an awesome time diving into *Culture Shock* with us, and we pray that God is speaking mightily to you through these sessions! Here are some questions and final thoughts that will help pull together the convictions we believe God wants for a set-apart generation—a generation of young people who are committed to integrity and purity.

CINDERELLA LIED, SUPERMAN DIED

When you look back to the Cinderella Lied session, what lies did you identify that you were believing about yourself? Have any more come to mind since that time? List three, or more, that you want to continue praying about.

BRACE FOR IMPACT

When your group talked about media choices, were you able to develop a game plan for your future response for the time when you'll be placed in a tough spot regarding media? What was it? Have you had the chance to exercise some of your Culture Shock thinking about your media choices? How's it going?

THE POPULARITY CONTEST

Can you see any ways you've hurt other people in your quest for popularity, even though you felt your actions were justified? The next time someone hurts you, how do you think you'll respond? How has considering what it means to be a real friend changed your attitude toward others?

FEARLESS PURITY

Walking in purity is more than just not having sex. It's about developing a lifestyle that honors God in heart, mind, and body. Are you committed to keeping your heart and mind pure? Since the time that you went through the Fearless Purity session, what has come up that has challenged or might challenge your stand for purity? How are you handling the temptation? Write down three things that you're committed to doing in order to stay pure.

ESCAPING NORMAL

Since the need in this world is so great, sometimes the idea of serving seems daunting. But really, you can start with the little things, like doing the dishes for your mom or dad or picking up trash around your school. What are three small things you can start doing? Remember, it might not change your world overnight, but you'll be setting an awesome example for those around you, plus totally blessing your parents!

Final thoughts from our team:

We're rooting for you! This survival guide was written by people who are facing all the same challenges you are. We've all made mistakes and all had to seek God seriously to help us create change in our lives. This road of revolution isn't easy, but it's surprisingly full of joy. When we live for ourselves, it actually makes us unhappy. If you try it for any length of time, you'll know what we mean. But every time we choose to do things God's way, our lives actually get better and fuller.

People may question your standards, and even give you a hard time about them. But just remember: being able to stand pure before God, able to say "Yes, I did it—I kept my promises" is worth everything. And if marriage is in God's plan for you, there will be no better feeling than the peace of mind you have when you can look into the eyes of your husband or wife on your wedding day, able to say "I've kept myself pure for you."

So don't let anyone make you lose sight of your goals! Commit to purity and integrity. Take a stand for a life lived uncompromisingly for God.

NOTES

1. Ron Luce, *Recreate Your World: Find Your Voice, Shape the Culture, Change the World* (Ventura, CA: Regal, 2008), 121.
2. Craig Gross and Steven Luff, *Pure Eyes: A Man's Guide to Sexual Integrity* (Grand Rapids, MI: Baker, 2010), 74, 78–79.
3. Craig Gross with Jason Harper, *Eyes of Integrity: The Porn Pandemic and How It Affects You* (Grand Rapids, MI: Baker, 2010), 21.
4. Stephen Arterburn and Fred Stoeker with Mike Yorkey, *Every Man's Battle: Winning the War on Sexual Temptation One Victory at a Time* (Colorado Springs, CO: WaterBrook Press, 2009), 92.
5. Herbert B. Swope, American journalist, http://thinkexist.com.
6. *Webster's American Dictionary of the English Language,* 1828 edition, http://1828. mshaffer.com/d/search/word,virtue.
7. Max Lucado, *Outlive Your Life: You Were Made to Make a Difference* (Nashville, TN: Thomas Nelson, 2010), 14.
8. C. S. Lewis, *Mere Christianity* from *The Complete C. S. Lewis Signature Classics* (San Francisco: HarperSanFrancisco, 2002), 69.

ABOUT GENERATIONS OF VIRTUE

The Generations of Virtue team probably isn't what you'd expect. We're just your average globe-trotting, coffee-addicted Jesus freaks who are passionate about spreading God's message of purity and holiness to youth, parents, and pretty much anyone who will listen. When we aren't on the road, we live, work, and play in Colorado Springs, Colorado.

To find out more about us and our mission, programs, resources, and publications, go to www.generationsofvirtue.org. To keep up with our crazy adventures and to connect with our team, head over to www.apuregeneration.com.

Pictured (L to R): Katherine Lockhart, Timothy Warner, Julie Hiramine,
Courtney Alberson, Kelsey Roberts, Sara Raley, Isaac Roberts, and Megan Briggs.